SHOW MOM HOW

SHOW

MOM HOW

THE HANDBOOK FOR THE BRAND-NEW MOM

SARAH HINES STEPHENS

pregnancy
planning

baby care

fun and
games

prepare

1 know when you're ready
2 get ready to get pregnant
3 eat right to conceive
4 follow your fertility
5 get in position to conceive
6 try for a boy
7 try for a girl
8 understand conception
9 recognize signs of pregnancy
10 share the news
11 eat right for two
12 soar as a supermom-to-be
13 track baby development
14 read a sonogram
15 manage morning sickness
16 minimize swelling
17 ease aches and pains
18 avoid indigestion
19 sleep comfortably
20 stretch out in cat-cow pose
21 flex in cobbler pose
22 feel good in pigeon pose
23 feature your bump
24 keep your bump under wraps
25 make a 40-week plan
26 understand an epidural
27 set up a water birth
28 deliver by cesarean section

29 have a hypnobirth
30 avoid unwanted touching
31 do it while pregnant
32 feel sexy in your new shape
33 pamper yourself
34 mellow out with meditation
35 connect with your unborn baby
36 read baby's movements
37 read your bump
38 divine gender
39 celebrate your belly
40 cast your belly
41 prep the nursery
42 stock up for baby
43 tie a no-sew blanket
44 decorate a nursery with stencils
45 baby-proof your home
46 induce labor naturally
47 induce labor with acupressure
48 pack a bag for labor
49 deliver a baby in a taxi
50 bond after birth
51 read newborn markings
52 dress baby for homecoming
53 hold a new baby
54 stimulate your newborn
55 heal at home
56 plant a placenta

nurture

57 hold a hopi sunrise blessing
58 celebrate an orthodox baptism
59 have a red egg and ginger party
60 perform a yoruba blessing
61 stage a hindu naming ritual
62 name baby the egyptian way
63 ready your troops
64 keep visits safe and sweet

65 introduce baby to your pet
66 make a birth announcement
67 swaddle an infant
68 set up a nursing station
69 breast-feed a newborn
70 position baby for breast-feeding
71 nurse on the go
72 pump at work

73 ease engorgement
74 treat a blocked duct
75 heal cracked nipples
76 bottle-feed a baby
77 warm a bottle
78 burp a baby
79 change a diaper
80 pack a diaper bag
81 handle diaper disasters
82 soothe a crying infant
83 massage a colicky newborn
84 cut teething pain
85 freeze a teething treat

86 wind down for bedtime
87 troubleshoot sleeping issues
88 fake a clean house
89 do yoga with your baby
90 gently massage your baby
91 care for the cord
92 sponge-bathe an infant
93 bathe a baby
94 take baby's temperature
95 trim baby's nails
96 clean baby's gums
97 treat cradle cap
98 prevent diaper rash

99   soup up your stroller
100 work out in a park
101 blend up mushy food
102 manage mealtime
103 freeze baby food
104 feed finger foods
105 eat out with baby
106 take a car trip
107 stock your trunk for trips
108 travel by air
109 take care of yourself
110 soothe with aromatherapy

play

111 make baby laugh
112 stimulate early vision
113 play with your baby
114 roll up a boo-boo bunny
115 tackle tummy time
116 promote sitting up
117 encourage rolling over
118 strengthen with elbow stands
119 support a wheelbarrow
120 make a texture tag blanket
121 use a texture tag blanket
122 play hide-and-seek
123 play peekaboo
124 play patty-cake
125 shake things up
126 move to the music
127 help baby crawl
128 encourage walking
129 spot movement milestones

130 distract baby at the store
131 entertain baby in an audience
132 keep baby calm in a long line
133 put baby to work at the office
134 make a banana octopus
135 cut a puzzle sandwich
136 engage baby's senses
137 share a park playdate
138 make messy art
139 make a tiny handprint
140 paint under plastic wrap
141 paint with water
142 sew a cute hooded towel
143 have bathtime fun
144 play itsy-bitsy spider
145 make a baby-sock puppet
146 put on a puppet show
147 read with your baby
148 build language skills

149 learn animal signs
150 take a spring stroll
151 have fun in the summer sun
152 fall into autumn adventure
153 go for a winter wander
154 make housework fun
155 play airplane
156 bounce baby on your lap
157 build a boxcar
158 build, crash, kick, and roll
159 take great baby pictures
160 capture the moments
161 swing with a retro baby
162 mosh with a punk baby
163 go green with an eco baby
164 chill out with a hippie baby
165 turn sleeves into pants
166 celebrate the big one

a note from sarah

Prepare all you want (#25), but as the mother of two I can assure you that nobody is ever really ready to have a baby (#1). The second you reveal you are pregnant (#10), people will offer unsolicited advice. Sometimes this can be a great thing (#55). Other times, not so much (#30). Here is *my* best piece of advice: trust your instincts. From the moment you hear your baby's heartbeat (#14), feel her move inside you (#36), or gaze into her eyes for the first time (#50), nobody will know your baby (or your body) like you do. You are your own parenting expert. So listen to your feelings (#34), roll up your sleeves (#79), ask for help if you need it (#63), and don't forget to enjoy the ride (#106)!

10   share the news

79   change a diaper

63   ready your troops

SARAH is a mother, children's author, and gardening instructor who has built her share of cardboard boxcars (#157) and enjoyed some serious bathtime frolic (#143). After attending eight births (#48, #26) and giving birth twice (#29), she still can't quite get over the fact that we all arrive in this manner. Though her kids are now school-age, Sarah can still play a mean game of peekaboo (#123) and handle whatever life throws her way (#81). She would like to thank her momtourage and the best baby-daddy in Oakland for everything, always.

build a boxcar 157

have bathtime fun 143

pack a bag for labor 48

have a hypnobirth 29

play peekaboo 123

handle diaper disasters 81

how to use this book

In the pages that follow, virtually every piece of essential information is presented graphically. In most cases the pictures do, indeed, tell the whole story. In some cases though, you'll need a little extra information to get it done right. Here's how we present those facts.

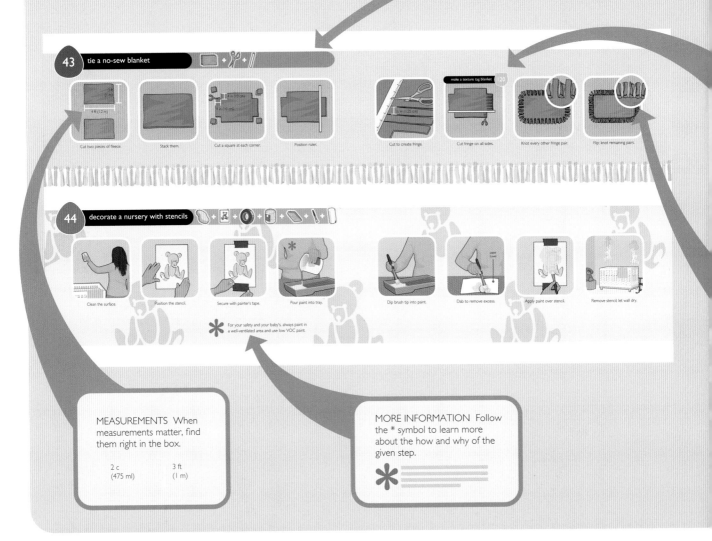

43 tie a no-sew blanket

Cut two pieces of fleece. | Stack them. | Cut a square at each corner. | Position ruler.

make a texture tag blanket 120

Cut to create fringe. | Cut fringe on all sides. | Knot every other fringe pair. | Flip; knot remaining pairs.

44 decorate a nursery with stencils

Clean the surface. | Position the stencil. | Secure with painter's tape. | Pour paint into tray. | Dip brush tip into paint. | Dab to remove excess. | Apply paint over stencil. | Remove stencil; let wall dry.

* For your safety and your baby's, always paint in a well-ventilated area and use low VOC paint.

MEASUREMENTS When measurements matter, find them right in the box.

2 c
(475 ml)

3 ft
(1 m)

MORE INFORMATION Follow the * symbol to learn more about the how and why of the given step.

TOOLS Everything you'll need to perform an activity appears in the toolbars. Having a hard time deciphering an item? Turn to the tools glossary in the back of the book.

CROSS-REFERENCES When one thing just leads to another, we'll point it out. Follow the links for related or interesting information.

make a texture tag blanket   120

ZOOMS These little circles zoom in on a step's important details, or depict the step's crucial "don'ts."

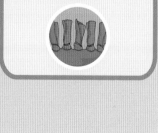

ICON GUIDE Throughout the book, handy icons show you just how it's done. Here are the icons you'll encounter.

 Check out the timer to learn how much time a relatively short task takes.

The calendar shows how many days, weeks, or months an activity requires.

 Look to the thermometer to learn the temperature needed for a given action.

 Repeat the depicted action the designated number of times.

Phew—fumes! Open a window before performing this activity.

 Just how hot, you ask? Cook over low, medium, or high heat, respectively.

SAFETY NOTES When doing the activities in this book, always take care to ensure that you and your child are safe. Keep these guidelines in mind:

- During and after pregnancy, consult a physician before attempting any activity involving physical exertion, or whenever your condition could impair or limit your ability to engage in an activity.

- Do not leave your child unattended, even for a brief moment, during any activity. Be particularly cautious when participating in any activity involving water because of the risk of drowning.

- Keep small items, such as coins and candy, out of baby's reach. An item smaller than 1¾ inches (4.5 cm), such as a latex balloon or piece of paper, is a choking hazard. A good rule of thumb: if it can fit through a toilet paper roll, it is not safe for play.

- Also make sure that any string is no longer than 7 inches (18 cm). Never leave your baby unattended with ribbons or strings, as they could pose a strangulation hazard.

- Before trying an activity, assess whether it's appropriate for your child's level of development. Use writing and crafts materials that are nontoxic and have been approved for your child's age.

- See #45 for tips on making your home safer for baby; for example, remove crib mobiles once your baby can push up onto hands and knees.

Let's just set aside for a sec the notion that anyone can ever really be ready emotionally for motherhood. But prepping physically before you get knocked up? Now that you can do. Eat right? Check. Vitamins? OK. Doctor visit? Will do. Have sex—a lot? Now we're talking! (Hey, it's all in the service of perpetuating the species.) Once doing the deed does the trick, your embryo will grow from a single cell to full-on human in 40 weeks, give or take. And while your baby is changing, so are you. You get it all! Morning sickness, kicks in the kidneys, and some unmentionable complaints, sure—but also super-shiny hair, strong nails, and va-va-voom cleavage. Meanwhile, you can also use this prep time to equip your house and lay in supplies for a newborn. All in anticipation of the day you can say to the newest member of your family: "Welcome home, baby."

prepare

I know when you're ready

You love spending time
with other people's kids.

Your personal finances
are in order.

65 introduce baby to your pet

You dote on your pets.

You have supportive friends
and family nearby.

You love looking at
(or buying!) baby stuff.

You think pregnant
women look beautiful.

You realize no one
is ever really ready!

Kick any bad habits.

Eat well.

Stay in shape.

Talk it over with a doctor.

Get dental work done.

Take prenatal vitamins.

Toss your birth control.

Get busy!

eat right to conceive 3

Leafy greens are full of iron, important for conception.

Monounsaturated fats help keep hormones balanced.

Plant-based proteins promote ovulation.

Citrus fruit contains folate, key for fetal development.

4 follow your fertility

There are several ways to track your fertility cycle and predict the best days for conception. Still having trouble? Consult a physician.

week 4

week 1

week 3

week 2

period

check your cervix

read your underwear

chart your temperature

check your cervix
Insert a clean finger toward the back of your vagina to feel your cervix.

read your underwear
The look and feel of your vaginal mucus can clue you in to fertile days.

chart your temperature
Take your basal body temperature before you get up in the morning.

low and hard cervix

"dry" days

low temperature

low temperature

"dry" days

low and hard cervix

basal temperature spike sustained for 48 hours

mucus the consistency of egg white

whitish discharge

high and soft cervix

fertile

fertile

ovulation

You can increase the odds of conceiving by choosing positions that allow for deep penetration and that deposit semen closer to the cervix.

Make missionary magic.

Get down on all fours.

Spoon.

Keep him on top.

Avoid standing positions.

Male sperm swim faster and die more quickly than female sperm. So if you want a boy, adjust your love-making routine to get those speedy Y chromosomes to a ready egg stat!

Eat potassium-rich foods.

Give him coffee before sex.

Use deep penetration.

Have sex after ovulation.

Sperm carrying the X chromosome travel more slowly to the egg and stay viable longer than Y-carrying sperm. If you want a girl, use conception conditions that favor these slow and steady sperm.

Eat magnesium-rich foods.

Have him take a bath first.

Make it missionary style.

Have sex before ovulation.

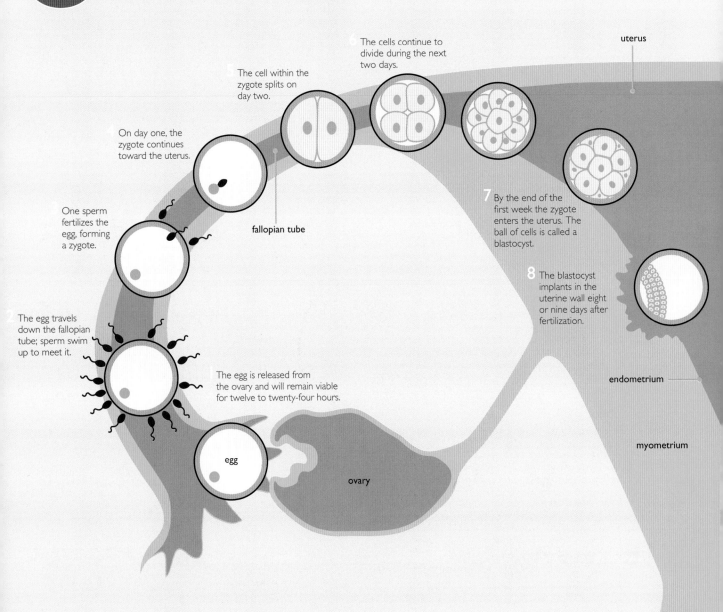

8 understand conception

Once a month, during ovulation, a mature egg is released from the ovaries. If it is fertilized on its way to the uterus, it will implant. If not, it will be shed along with the uterine lining.

6 The cells continue to divide during the next two days.

uterus

5 The cell within the zygote splits on day two.

4 On day one, the zygote continues toward the uterus.

fallopian tube

One sperm fertilizes the egg, forming a zygote.

7 By the end of the first week the zygote enters the uterus. The ball of cells is called a blastocyst.

8 The blastocyst implants in the uterine wall eight or nine days after fertilization.

2 The egg travels down the fallopian tube; sperm swim up to meet it.

The egg is released from the ovary and will remain viable for twelve to twenty-four hours.

endometrium

egg

ovary

myometrium

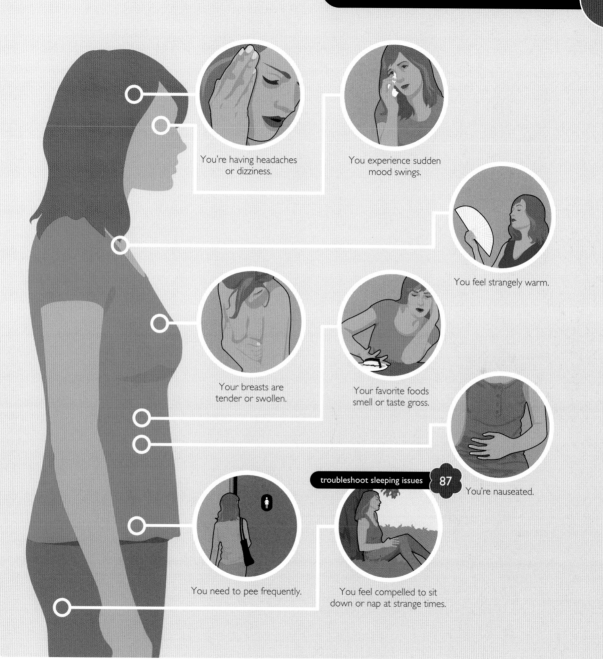

You're having headaches or dizziness.

You experience sudden mood swings.

You feel strangely warm.

Your breasts are tender or swollen.

Your favorite foods smell or taste gross.

troubleshoot sleeping issues **87**

You're nauseated.

You need to pee frequently.

You feel compelled to sit down or nap at strange times.

Savor the moment alone.

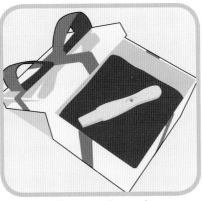
Wrap up positive proof.

Update your grocery list: eggs, milk, diapers.

Drop a hint.

Make a movie poster.

Send a sonogram.

Give a gift they can wear proudly.

77 warm a bottle

Put a message in a (baby) bottle.

Set an extra spot.

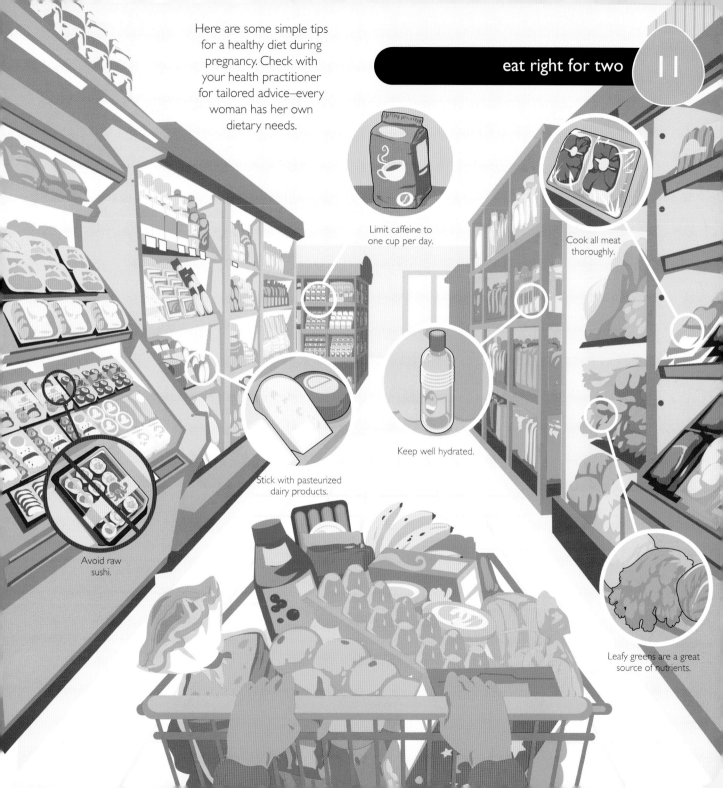

Here are some simple tips for a healthy diet during pregnancy. Check with your health practitioner for tailored advice—every woman has her own dietary needs.

eat right for two

Limit caffeine to one cup per day.

Cook all meat thoroughly.

Stick with pasteurized dairy products.

Keep well hydrated.

Avoid raw sushi.

Leafy greens are a great source of nutrients.

12 soar as a supermom-to-be

You have a bionic nose.

Your curves stop traffic.

Nails grow long and strong.

You have a supernatural glow.

13 track baby development

In nine months, your baby will grow from the size of a tiny seed to a round, ripe watermelon. Along the way, she'll develop vital organs and all of the little details, like teensy toenails, you'll soon be cooing over.

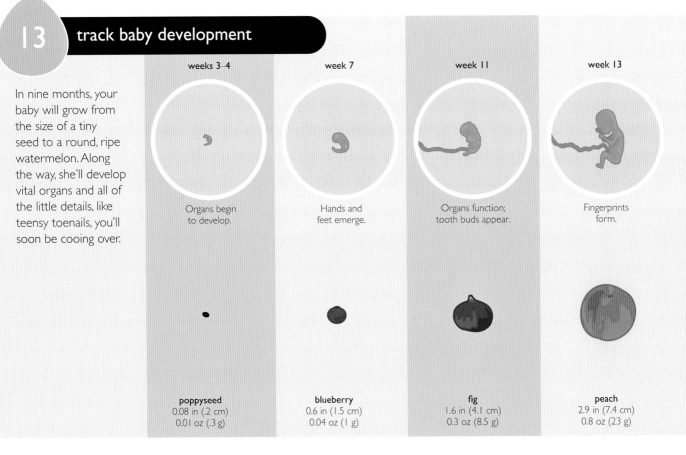

weeks 3–4	week 7	week 11	week 13
Organs begin to develop.	Hands and feet emerge.	Organs function; tooth buds appear.	Fingerprints form.
poppyseed 0.08 in (.2 cm) 0.01 oz (.3 g)	**blueberry** 0.6 in (1.5 cm) 0.04 oz (1 g)	**fig** 1.6 in (4.1 cm) 0.3 oz (8.5 g)	**peach** 2.9 in (7.4 cm) 0.8 oz (23 g)

Your hair is blindingly shiny.

Your heart is supersized.

You have surging emotions.

You can create new life!

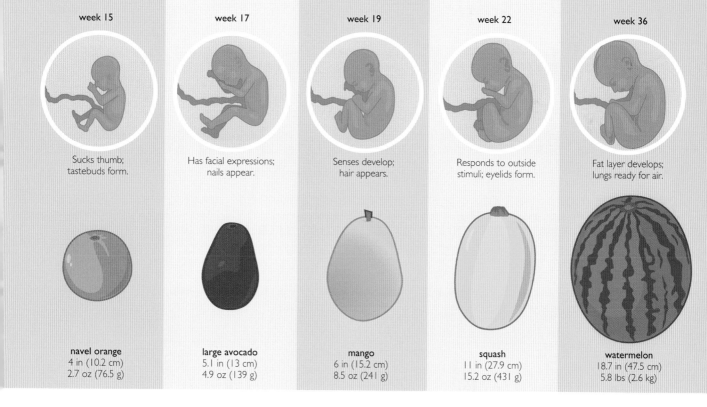

week 15

Sucks thumb; tastebuds form.

navel orange
4 in (10.2 cm)
2.7 oz (76.5 g)

week 17

Has facial expressions; nails appear.

large avocado
5.1 in (13 cm)
4.9 oz (139 g)

week 19

Senses develop; hair appears.

mango
6 in (15.2 cm)
8.5 oz (241 g)

week 22

Responds to outside stimuli; eyelids form.

squash
11 in (27.9 cm)
15.2 oz (431 g)

week 36

Fat layer develops; lungs ready for air.

watermelon
18.7 in (47.5 cm)
5.8 lbs (2.6 kg)

A sonogram (also known as an ultrasound) uses sound waves to "see" your baby. Here's some of the inside information this helpful procedure will reveal.

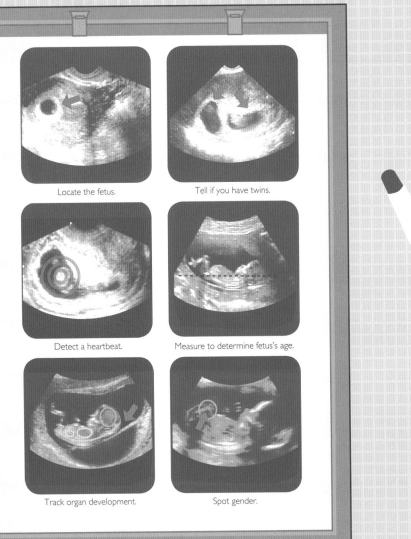

Locate the fetus.

Tell if you have twins.

Detect a heartbeat.

Measure to determine fetus's age.

Track organ development.

Spot gender.

Eat small, frequent, bland meals.

Have breakfast in bed.

Sniff refreshing scents.

Hydrate with lemon water.

Indulge your cravings.

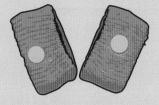

Wear sea bands.

Just in case tricks don't help, carry a kit for freshening up.

 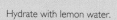

Wear low, wide heels.

Elevate your feet and legs.

Cut your salt intake.

Eat cucumbers and melons.

Stay hydrated.

Get a leg up when standing.

Bend toward the pain.

Apply creams to tight skin.

Support your lower back.

Firm your bed with a board.

Use a lavender compress.

Wear a supportive layer.

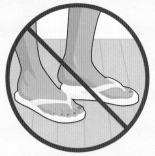

Ditch flat shoes.

Leave heavy lifting to others.

Stand up straight.

Avoid sudden moves.

Pass on spicy, fatty foods.

Separate fats and sweets.

Keep meals small.

Drink between meals.

Eat apples.

Ask your doctor about antacids.

Stay upright after eating.

Elevate with a wedge.

Keep it cool (and dark).

Sleep on your left side.

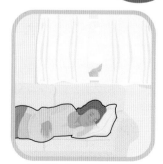
Use pillows for support.

Take frequent naps.

20 stretch out in cat-cow pose

Place wrists below shoulders and knees below hips.

Inhale, curl toes under, drop belly slightly, gaze up.

Exhale, press tops of feet down, round spine, drop head.

Repeat steps two and three.

21 flex in cobbler pose

Sit with back straight.

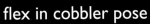

Bring soles of feet together.

Gently lower knees; press feet together.

For an advanced stretch, lean forward slightly.

22 feel good in pigeon pose

Place right foot on left knee; flex right foot.

Place hands palm up on right leg.

Lean forward, stretching hips.

Breathe; sit back. Repeat with left leg.

Try easy tops in fun colors.

Get stylish jackets for work.

Go grown-up and sexy.

Get a big little black dress.

Load on lightweight layers.

Show off in a slinky top.

Unzip your favorite jacket.

Bare it all in a bikini.

Crossed bandages can help tame a bulging belly button.

Wear loose tunics.

Extend your old jeans.

Distract with jewelry.

Try V-necks in dark colors.

25 make a 40-week plan

Forty weeks seems like a long time, but your due date will arrive before you know it. Take care of as many details as possible before the big day, so you can focus on your baby afterward.

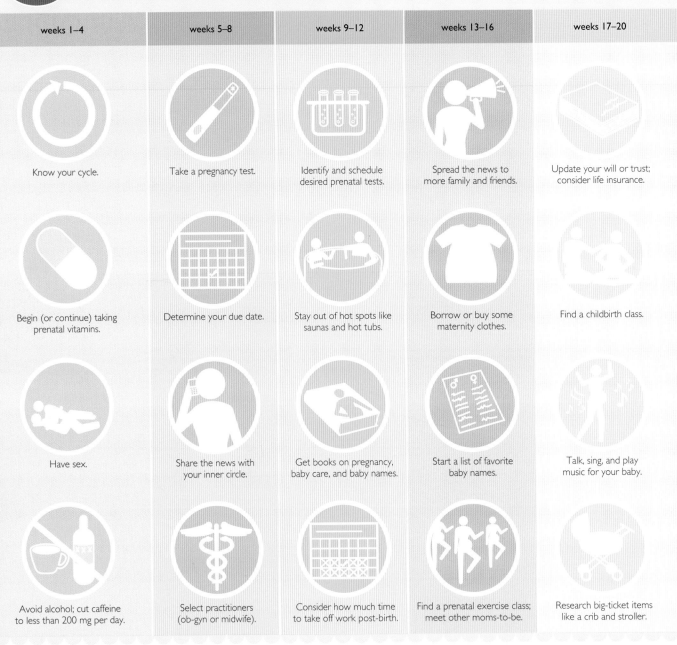

weeks 1–4	weeks 5–8	weeks 9–12	weeks 13–16	weeks 17–20
Know your cycle.	Take a pregnancy test.	Identify and schedule desired prenatal tests.	Spread the news to more family and friends.	Update your will or trust; consider life insurance.
Begin (or continue) taking prenatal vitamins.	Determine your due date.	Stay out of hot spots like saunas and hot tubs.	Borrow or buy some maternity clothes.	Find a childbirth class.
Have sex.	Share the news with your inner circle.	Get books on pregnancy, baby care, and baby names.	Start a list of favorite baby names.	Talk, sing, and play music for your baby.
Avoid alcohol; cut caffeine to less than 200 mg per day.	Select practitioners (ob-gyn or midwife).	Consider how much time to take off work post-birth.	Find a prenatal exercise class; meet other moms-to-be.	Research big-ticket items like a crib and stroller.

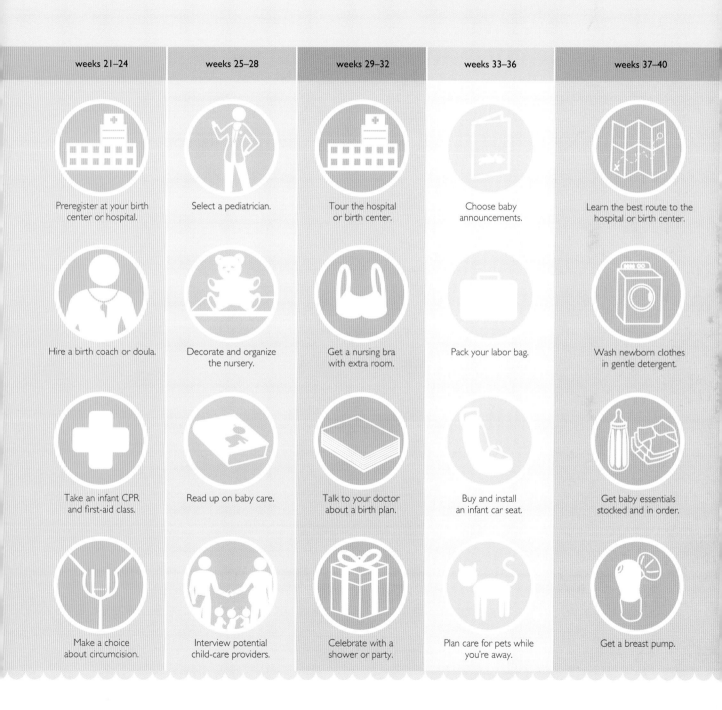

weeks 21–24	weeks 25–28	weeks 29–32	weeks 33–36	weeks 37–40
Preregister at your birth center or hospital.	Select a pediatrician.	Tour the hospital or birth center.	Choose baby announcements.	Learn the best route to the hospital or birth center.
Hire a birth coach or doula.	Decorate and organize the nursery.	Get a nursing bra with extra room.	Pack your labor bag.	Wash newborn clothes in gentle detergent.
Take an infant CPR and first-aid class.	Read up on baby care.	Talk to your doctor about a birth plan.	Buy and install an infant car seat.	Get baby essentials stocked and in order.
Make a choice about circumcision.	Interview potential child-care providers.	Celebrate with a shower or party.	Plan care for pets while you're away.	Get a breast pump.

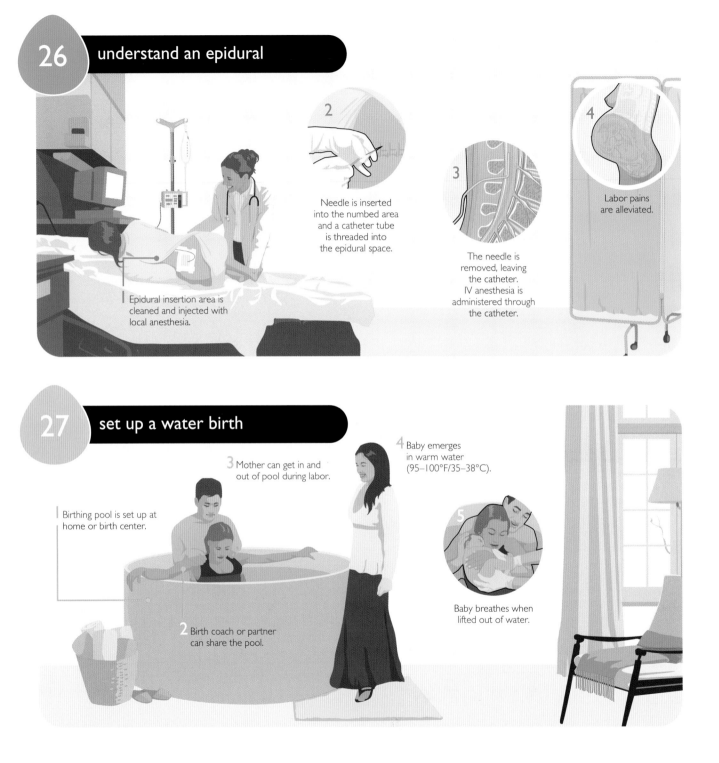

26 understand an epidural

Epidural insertion area is cleaned and injected with local anesthesia.

2 Needle is inserted into the numbed area and a catheter tube is threaded into the epidural space.

3 The needle is removed, leaving the catheter. IV anesthesia is administered through the catheter.

4 Labor pains are alleviated.

27 set up a water birth

Birthing pool is set up at home or birth center.

2 Birth coach or partner can share the pool.

3 Mother can get in and out of pool during labor.

4 Baby emerges in warm water (95–100°F/35–38°C).

5 Baby breathes when lifted out of water.

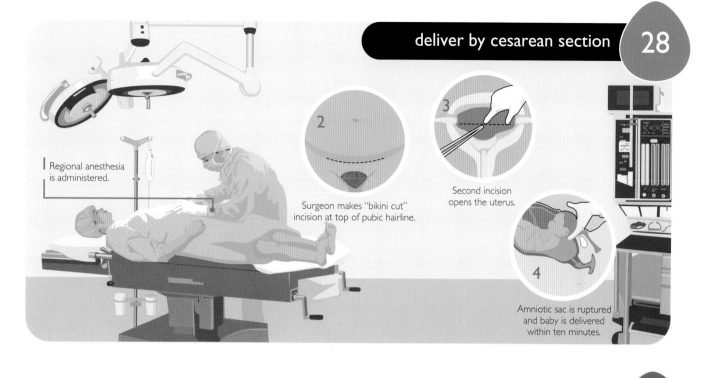

1 Regional anesthesia is administered.

2 Surgeon makes "bikini cut" incision at top of pubic hairline.

3 Second incision opens the uterus.

4 Amniotic sac is ruptured and baby is delivered within ten minutes.

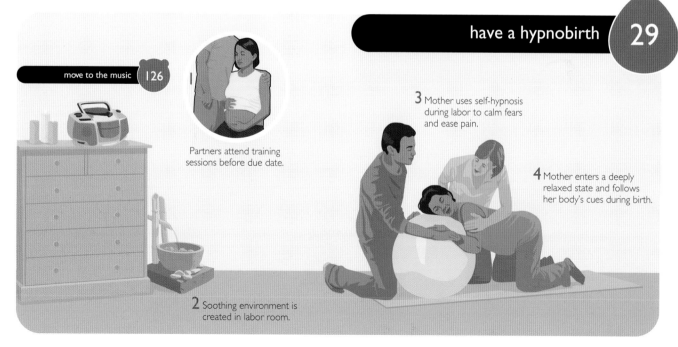

move to the music 126

1 Partners attend training sessions before due date.

2 Soothing environment is created in labor room.

3 Mother uses self-hypnosis during labor to calm fears and ease pain.

4 Mother enters a deeply relaxed state and follows her body's cues during birth.

30 avoid unwanted touching

Keep a protective hand on your belly.

Let your belly do the talking.

Shoulder-block potential gropers.

31 do it while pregnant

Spoon.

Get on top.

Take the pressure off.

Go manual.

Back away slowly.

Give them a taste of their own medicine.

Threaten to scream if touched.

Work your new curves.

Let him know how you feel.

Get close and cuddly.

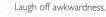

Laugh off awkwardness.

Hormones and body changes may make you feel sexier than ever, or awkward and uncomfortable . . . or both! Ebbs and flows are completely normal. The important thing is to do what feels good.

Indulge in prenatal massage.

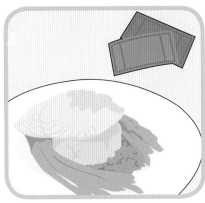

Treat yourself to dinner and a movie.

Spend time with friends.

Get away for a weekend.

Dive in and take a load off!

Talk to other moms and moms-to-be.

Have your hair cut or styled.

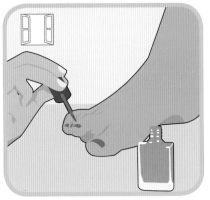

Get your nails done with chemical-free polish.

Tune out unwanted advice.

Surround yourself with soothing, spiritual items, then sit comfortably. Relax and let your inhalations and exhalations roll through you. If thoughts occur to you, simply acknowledge them, and return your attention to your breath.

If a sound distracts you, mentally label it "noise" and return to your breath.

If you feel worry, frustration, or any other emotion (even a positive one), think "emotion" to yourself and return to your breath.

If you catch yourself planning or thinking about the future, say "thought" to yourself and return to your breath.

If you experience an itch, tickle, or kick, think "physical sensation" and return to your breath.

In addition to making you feel calmer and more connected to your body, meditation has important health benefits for you and your child. A meditation practice of even a few minutes per day can help reduce stress hormones.

Studies show that babies recognize voices and music that they heard before they were born. Early sounds may influence musical taste and language ability.

Listening to your baby's heartbeat can make you feel instantly connected.

Relax and visualize your baby. The calm feelings will soothe you both.

Massaging your belly releases relaxing hormones.

Share your favorite tunes with your baby.

Read out loud and sing! Babies show a preference for voices they heard in utero.

Invite loved ones to talk to your baby. Their familiar voices will be soothing later.

When you feel your baby is active, tap out a rhythm and wait for a response.

Pow! Whap! What's that baby doing in there? Every baby has different patterns and frequencies of movement, usually starting around eighteen weeks and then slowing down a few weeks before birth. Here are some actions you might feel.

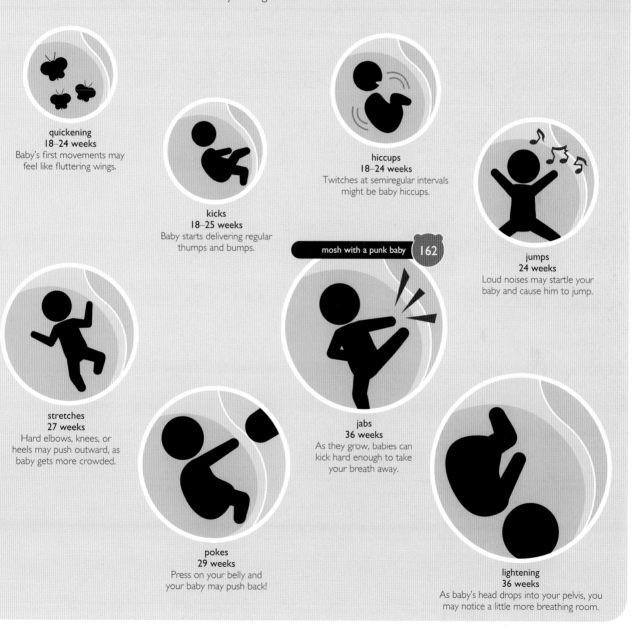

quickening
18–24 weeks
Baby's first movements may feel like fluttering wings.

kicks
18–25 weeks
Baby starts delivering regular thumps and bumps.

hiccups
18–24 weeks
Twitches at semiregular intervals might be baby hiccups.

jumps
24 weeks
Loud noises may startle your baby and cause him to jump.

mosh with a punk baby 162

stretches
27 weeks
Hard elbows, knees, or heels may push outward, as baby gets more crowded.

jabs
36 weeks
As they grow, babies can kick hard enough to take your breath away.

pokes
29 weeks
Press on your belly and your baby may push back!

lightening
36 weeks
As baby's head drops into your pelvis, you may notice a little more breathing room.

read your bump

An amniocentesis and ultrasound will tell you for sure, but you can have fun using old wives' tales to guess your baby's gender.

boy

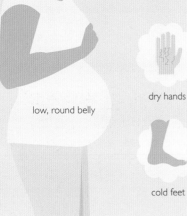

low, round belly

dry hands

craving protein

cold feet

prefer to lie on left side

girl

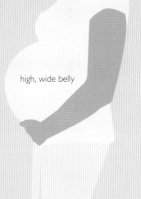

soft hands

craving fruit and chocolate

hairier legs

prefer to lie on right side

high, wide belly

---

divine gender

Tie a charm to a long string.

Suspend it over your belly.

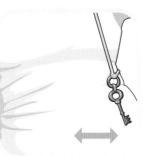

Back-and-forth means "boy."

A circle means "girl."

celebrate your belly 39

Record feelings in a journal.

Take up belly dancing.

name baby the egyptian way 62

Get a henna "tattoo."

Have boudoir photos taken.

cast your belly 40

Cut bandages into triangles.

Mix plaster of paris.

Coat skin in petroleum jelly.

Dip strips in plaster; apply.

Work quickly to cover belly.

Cover breasts last.

Let dry.

Decorate and display.

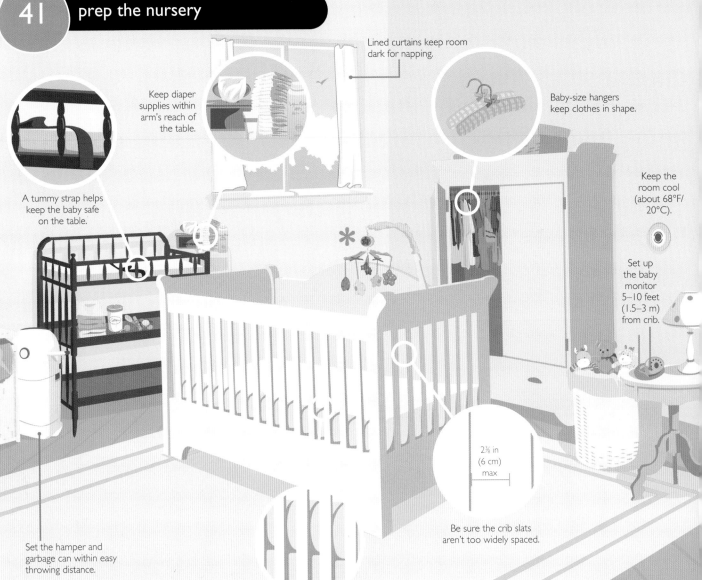

Lined curtains keep room dark for napping.

Keep diaper supplies within arm's reach of the table.

Baby-size hangers keep clothes in shape.

A tummy strap helps keep the baby safe on the table.

Keep the room cool (about 68°F/ 20°C).

Set up the baby monitor 5–10 feet (1.5–3 m) from crib.

2⅜ in (6 cm) max

Be sure the crib slats aren't too widely spaced.

Set the hamper and garbage can within easy throwing distance.

The mattress should press firmly against the rails. Sheets should fit snugly. Remove extra blankets, toys, and pillows from the crib.

Hang the mobile at least 1½ feet (.5 m) beyond the baby's reach. Remove as soon as the baby can push up on two hands.

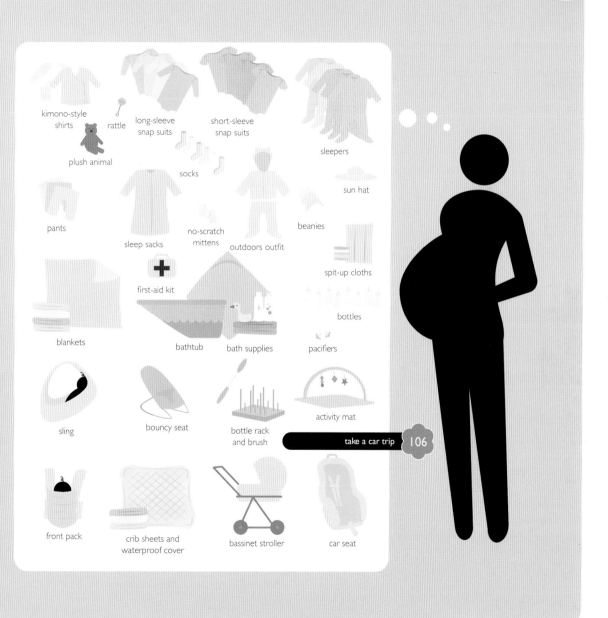

kimono-style shirts

rattle

plush animal

long-sleeve snap suits

short-sleeve snap suits

sleepers

socks

sun hat

pants

sleep sacks

no-scratch mittens

outdoors outfit

beanies

spit-up cloths

first-aid kit

bottles

blankets

bathtub

bath supplies

pacifiers

sling

bouncy seat

bottle rack and brush

activity mat

take a car trip 106

front pack

crib sheets and waterproof cover

bassinet stroller

car seat

43   tie a no-sew blanket

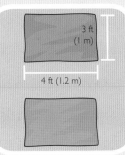
Cut two pieces of fleece.

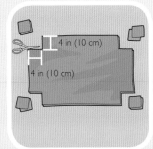
Stack them.

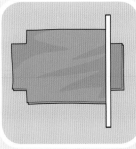
Cut a square at each corner.

Position ruler.

44   decorate a nursery with stencils

Clean the surface.

Position the stencil.

Secure with painter's tape.

Pour paint into tray.

For your safety and your baby's, always paint in a well-ventilated area and use low VOC paint.

Cut to create fringe.

Cut fringe on all sides.

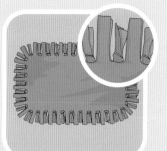

Knot every other fringe pair.

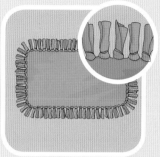

Flip; knot remaining pairs.

Dip brush tip into paint.

paper towel

Dab to remove excess.

Apply paint over stencil.

Remove stencil; let wall dry.

The key to baby-proofing is to think like a baby. Get down on the floor and crawl around for a baby's-eye view of household hazards. Repeat as your baby gets bigger and more mobile.

Place a nonslip mat in the tub.

Strap bookcases to the wall.

Install a toilet lock.

Unplug appliances. Store up high, along with all medicines.

Set water heater to 120°F (49°C).

Store cleaners out of reach.

Secure cords behind a cord fence.

Pad sharp corners on low furniture.

Tie window-blind cords out of reach.

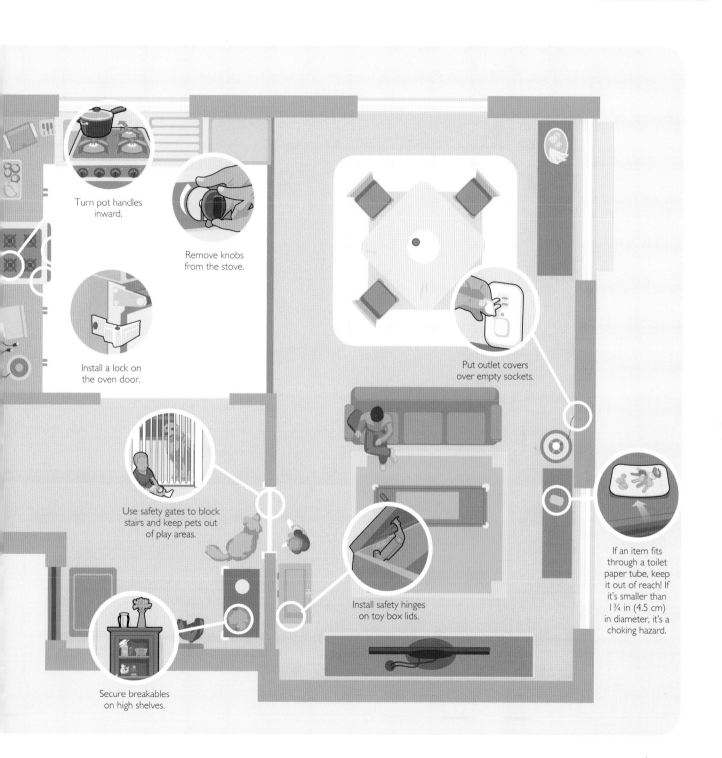

Turn pot handles inward.

Remove knobs from the stove.

Install a lock on the oven door.

Put outlet covers over empty sockets.

Use safety gates to block stairs and keep pets out of play areas.

If an item fits through a toilet paper tube, keep it out of reach! If it's smaller than 1¾ in (4.5 cm) in diameter, it's a choking hazard.

Install safety hinges on toy box lids.

Secure breakables on high shelves.

46   induce labor naturally

 These natural ways to induce labor should only be attempted when you have reached full-term (forty weeks). Always check with your doctor first.

Eat tropical or spicy foods.

4 tbsp castor oil
1 c (240 ml) water

Mix up a castor-oil cocktail.

Take a walk.

Get help from baby's daddy.

47   induce labor with acupressure

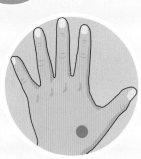

Pinch and rub webbing between your thumb and index finger.

Apply firm pressure to the spot four finger-widths above the ankle bone.

Find the point where the trapezius muscle connects to the neck. Measure down four finger-widths and apply intermittent firm pressure.

Gently massage your nipples to stimulate contractions.

When you head to the hospital, you'll want some comforts from home. Pack a small bag for the mom-to-be, and let the support person lug around the rest of the gear!

pen and paper

pillows with distinctive cases

contact list

map of hospital area

cell phone and charger

cash and coins for vending machines

massage oil and tennis ball

mp3 player and dock

diaper bag

grooming items

shampoo and deodorant

toothpaste and toothbrushes

watch

snacks

car seat

extra blankets

camera and batteries

change of clothes

support person

shampoo and deodorant

sanitary wipes

hard candy

makeup

eyewear and supplies

lip balm

soap and hand lotion

hair-care items

nursing bra

labor clothes

change of clothes

medical documents

extra underwear

clothes to wear home

slip-on shoes

mom-to-be

deliver a baby in a taxi

Stop that taxi!

Crouch. Use gravity.

Gently catch the baby.

Wipe the baby's face.

Tie off the umbilical cord.

Hold close and keep warm.

Breast-feed if possible.

Hurry to the hospital!

TAXI

Cuddle skin-to-skin immediately after birth.

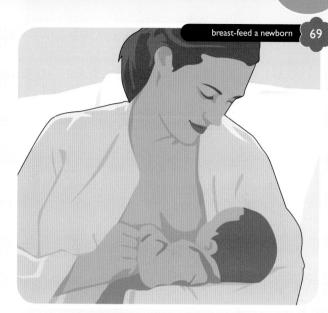

Nurse or offer a bottle while holding her close.

Make eye contact even though she can't focus.

Sing, coo, or speak. Your voice will already be familiar.

read newborn markings

Every baby is beautiful, but don't be alarmed if your newborn arrives with some unexpected fuzz, bumps, or marks.

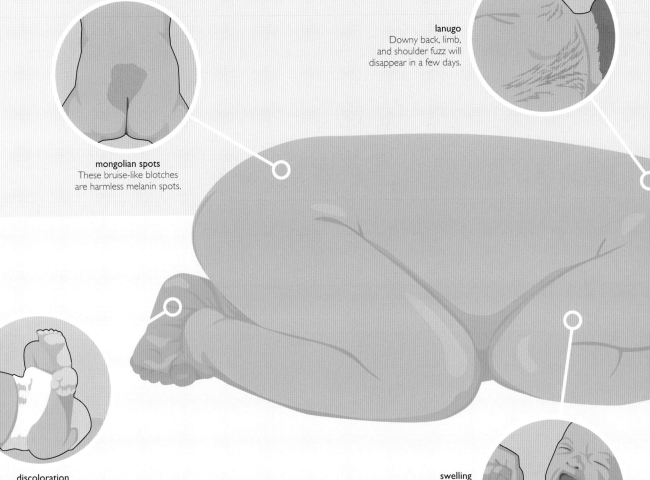

lanugo
Downy back, limb, and shoulder fuzz will disappear in a few days.

mongolian spots
These bruise-like blotches are harmless melanin spots.

discoloration
Blue hands and feet will turn rosy as baby's circulation strengthens.

swelling
Swollen breasts and genitals are the result of mom's hormones.

Keep clothing from rubbing the umbilicus.

vernix
This thick white substance protects baby's skin in amniotic fluid.

molding
The tight trip through the birth canal can elongate the head. It will shape up in a day or two.

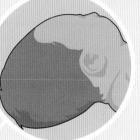

Opt for soft, loose clothing.

stork bites
Pink or red patches will fade over time.

Keep her warm with a hat.

milia
Tiny white spots, or baby acne, are caused by trapped oils.

squished features
Puffy eyes and flattened noses are only temporary.

Pack a blanket and spare outfit.

hold a new baby

Different baby holds are useful in different situations. The belly hold is good for gas, while the cradle hold works well for soothing baby to sleep.

cradle hold

football hold

belly hold

shoulder hold

No matter which hold you use, remember to support baby's head with your hand or arm until she develops good neck strength.

54 stimulate your newborn

Hold him during chores.

Wear him out.

112 stimulate early vision

Captivate him with contrast.

Sing and talk to him.

Stay in your pajamas.

Accept help; don't host.

Ignore the phone and door.

Let go of doing it all.

Use a sitz bath to ease pain.

Stay hydrated. Eat fiber.

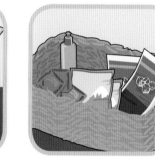

Keep a kit in the bathroom.

Sleep when the baby sleeps.

plant a placenta 56

Dig a hole in your yard.

Add placenta; cover with dirt.

Plant a seedling in the hole.

Watch tree and baby grow.

Yes, they did it—those hospital nurses actually let you take home this tiny stranger who miraculously emerged from your body (no, you did not dream that part). And yes, you can take care of her, even if your early swaddling efforts would get you laughed out of maternity-nurse school and you keep confusing the carseat LATCH system with a proper nursing latch. Now begins the endless laundry, a hormonal roller coaster that puts PMS to shame, and the kind of sleep deprivation that makes college all-nighters seem like, well, child's play. Even if you feel like you're all thumbs at first, you will figure out what works for your baby (promise!). So, what makes this 24/7 job worthwhile? You'll know when your baby first smiles at you, takes her first steps to you, and says "mama" for the first time.

nurture

57 hold a hopi sunrise blessing

Give baby her first name and introduce her to nature and society.

While indoors, baby rests between two perfectly formed ears of corn.

After spending her first nineteen days indoors, baby greets the sun and learns her name.

Baby's new name will last until age twenty-one, when she'll receive her adult name.

58 celebrate an orthodox baptism

This ritual welcomes baby into her church community.

Parents and godparents agree to bring baby up within the church.

Baby wears a white christening gown.

The priest anoints baby with oil and immerses her three times in water that has been blessed.

59 have a red egg and ginger party

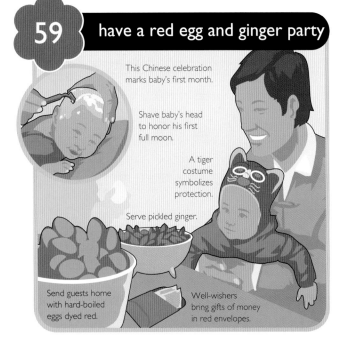

This Chinese celebration marks baby's first month.

Shave baby's head to honor his first full moon.

A tiger costume symbolizes protection.

Serve pickled ginger.

Send guests home with hard-boiled eggs dyed red.

Well-wishers bring gifts of money in red envelopes.

60 perform a yoruba blessing

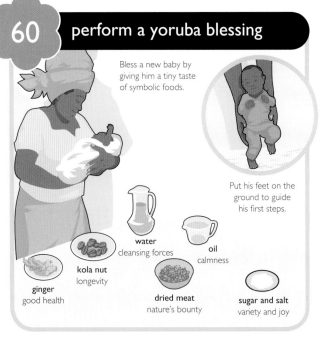

Bless a new baby by giving him a tiny taste of symbolic foods.

Put his feet on the ground to guide his first steps.

water
cleansing forces

oil
calmness

kola nut
longevity

ginger
good health

dried meat
nature's bounty

sugar and salt
variety and joy

Dress baby with new cloth.

Apply vermilion to foil evil.

Show baby a rising sun.

Honor the earth.

Reveal baby's name.

Have relatives greet baby.

Introduce baby to nature.

Father tells baby his name.

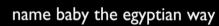

Clothe baby in white.

Pair names and candles.

Light candles; wait.

Final lit candle reveals name.

Invite parents when
you'll need them most.

Grandparents' expert
arms can give you a break.

Don't hesitate to put
well-wishers to work.

Welcome healthy children and
experienced moms to visit.

Make time for your new family
to bond without extra visitors.

Ask a friend to coordinate
meal deliveries and field calls.

Take care of the baby while friends
take care of errands and chores.

Connect with community or church
groups that offer support for new families.

If you can afford it, call in the pros.
A doula, cleaner, or grocery delivery
service can be worth the cost.

Ask visitors to wash up.

Place baby in waiting arms.

Lay baby in little laps.

Invite children to touch toes.

Expose pet to other kids.

Offer baby's clothes for a sniff.

Greet pet; bring in baby.

Hold baby; reassure pet.

Write it in the sky.

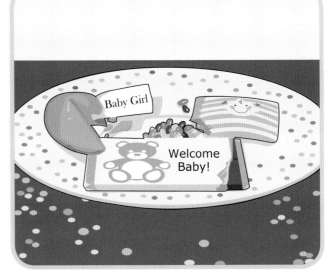

Tell the world tastefully with personalized treats.

Let the happy news travel in a fake passport.

Shout it from the rooftops.

Swaddling can pacify baby in the first
month by reminding her of the snug,
warm environment of the womb.

1

2

3

4

5

An adjustable light with a dimmer makes reading and snoozing easier.

A rocking chair with arms is good for supporting mom's elbows and baby's head. Pillows and blankets provide extra propping support.

Store nursing pads, creams, burp cloths, and grooming items where you'll need them.

Keep water, remotes, phone, books, and snacks within easy reach.

An adjustable stool is great for leg support.

Make skin-to-skin contact.

Find a comfortable hold.

Squeeze out a drop or two.

Wait for mouth to open.

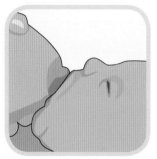

Bring baby in chin first.

Lips flare out.

Cover areola with latch.

Break seal to readjust.

It may take a while for you and your baby to get the hang of breast-feeding. Seek help right away if you are experiencing pain, anxiety, or frustration.

70 position baby for breast-feeding

basic cradle hold

cross-cradle hold

football or clutch hold

71 nurse on the go

Wear an easy-to-open bra.

Dress in stretchy tops.

Feed baby before he gets fussy.

Find a comfortable spot.

side-lying position

double football hold

double cradle hold

Put your feet up.

Nurse newborns in a sling.

Block out distractions.

Grab a booth when dining.

72 pump at work

Create a private space.

Stick to a schedule.

Remind yourself of baby.

Enjoy calming distractions.

Rub flanges with lanolin.

Lean in; let gravity assist.

Pump both breasts at once.

Keep cool (up to 24 hours).

73 ease engorgement

Cool with cold cabbage leaves.

Apply heat before nursing.

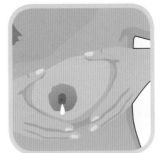
Express to relieve tightness.

Nurse regularly.

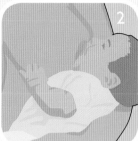
Identify sore, hard spot.

Nurse frequently to drain.

Apply warm compresses.

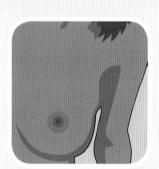
Massage in a steamy shower.

✱ If you are experiencing shooting pains in your breasts, or if nipple cracks are not healing, consult your health practitioner immediately.

heal cracked nipples 75

lanolin nipple cream

Apply before, after nursing.

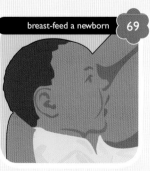
breast-feed a newborn 69

Check your latch.

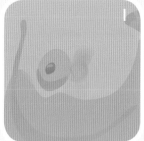
Air-dry after feeding.

Change nursing pads often.

76 bottle-feed a baby

Sterilize before initial use. Check the flow rate. Hold the bottle, don't prop. Angle to avoid air bubbles.

 New babies need nipples that offer a slow flow rate.
Many babies prefer faster flow rates as they get older.

77 warm a bottle

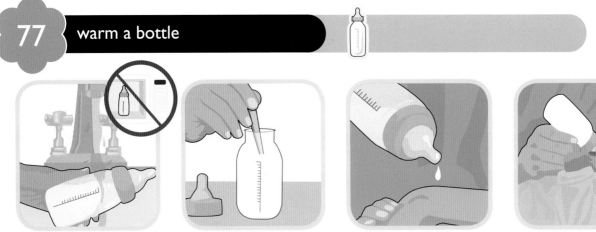

Hold under warm water. Stir to even temperature. Check that it's warm, not hot. Nourish!

Burp during and after meal.

Alternate sides.

Wash in dishwasher or hand wash.

Replace nipple when worn.

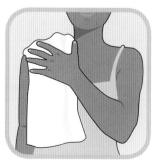

Place a burp cloth.

Position baby.

Rub or pat baby's back . . .

. . . until burp is achieved!

change a diaper

Lay baby on a flat surface. Strap in if needed.

Keep him covered to avoid being sprayed.

Wipe down, collecting mess.

Set diaper aside.

Keep feet and bottom elevated.

Wipe from front to back; don't forget skin folds.

Tuck used wipes in messy diaper.

Place fresh diaper under baby; apply cream as needed.

Secure diaper; fit should be snug, not tight.

Seal the mess with tabs; dispose.

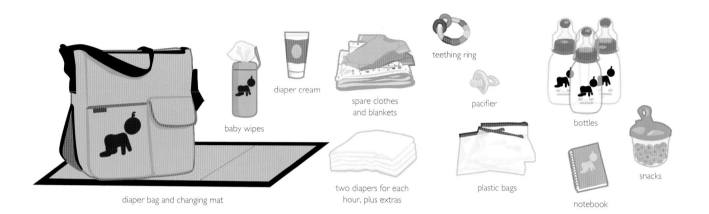

diaper cream

baby wipes

spare clothes
and blankets

teething ring

pacifier

bottles

snacks

notebook

plastic bags

two diapers for each
hour, plus extras

diaper bag and changing mat

Blowouts? Try a larger
diaper, or switch brands.

Improvise a changing station
on any available surface.

Contain a mess by using
your coat to swaddle.

To prevent
nighttime
leaks, put
a larger
diaper over a
smaller one.

Is baby prone
to removing or
reaching into his
diaper? Try tape.

Keep a bucket of
soapy water accessible
to pre-soak clothes.

82 soothe a crying infant

See if she needs a change.

Make sure clothes are loose.

Change location; go outside.

Sway to music.

Run the vacuum (or dryer).

Try a new hold.

Hold her close; hum a tune.

make baby laugh

Try some mirror magic.

83 massage a colicky newborn

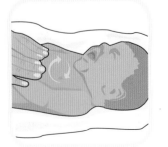
Stroke tummy clockwise.

Move his legs side to side.

Cycle those legs!

Press his knees in.

1 tbsp olive oil
4 drops clove oil

Mix; rub on sore gums.

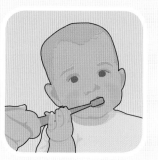

Offer a soft toothbrush.

Try teething biscuits.

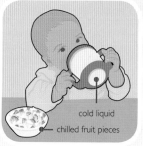

cold liquid

chilled fruit pieces

Chill out with cold treats.

 Teething biscuits or fruit pieces should only be used for older babies who are already used to finger foods.

freeze a teething treat 85

Brew chamomile tea.

washcloth

Knot; dip knot in the tea.

Freeze.

Give to your teething baby.

Start at the same time.

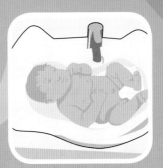

Soothe with a warm bath.

Fill baby's belly.

Change wet or dirty diapers.

Darken the room.

Share a story or song.

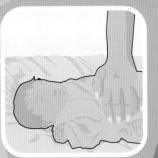

Lay on back; pat gently.

Use your ritual anywhere.

You may get a little tired of doing the same thing, but a consistent bedtime ritual signals to your baby that it's time for sleep and can help him settle down for the night. Once you've established your own pattern, try to stick with it.

Create some white noise.

Napping upright can prevent reflux.

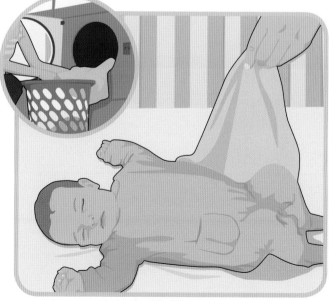

A warm towel takes the chill off. Remove it once he's asleep.

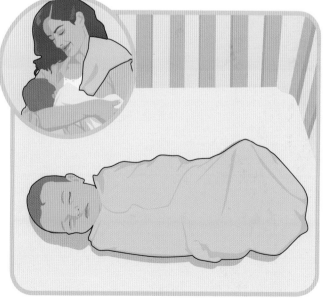

Securely swaddle him in something that smells like you.

fake a clean house

Having company over? Ten minutes is all it takes to fake a bit of better housekeeping.

Open a window to freshen things up.

Distract visitors with your adorable offspring!

Flip couch cushions. Use throw blankets or pillows to hide stains.

"Store" all your toiletries and towels behind the shower curtain.

Give surfaces a quick wipe with a damp cloth.

To make your clutter disappear, throw it all in a room and close the door. Magic!

The washer and dryer are great hiding spots.

Stash dirty dishes in the dishwasher or freezer.

Simmer cinnamon and cloves on the stove.

Empty trash bins that hold dirty diapers.

Vacuum a quick path through the house.

1 Place baby at top of mat.

2 Lift hips and straighten knees.

3 Bring heels down without straining.

4 Return to knees; kiss baby.

1 Sit with baby between legs.

2 Inhale and stretch up from the hips.

3 Exhale and reach forward.

4 Inhale to sit up; clap.

155 play airplane

Save this stretch until baby can hold her head up by herself (around four months).

1 Bring baby onto your shins.

2 Hold baby; lower torso.

3 Bring shins up.

4 Touch foreheads.

Lay baby on a blanket; cover body.

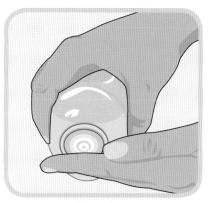

Oil your hands.

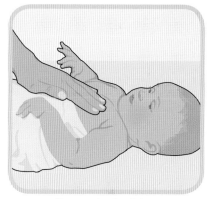

Keep one hand on baby.

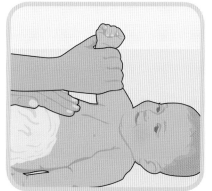

Use slow milking motions.

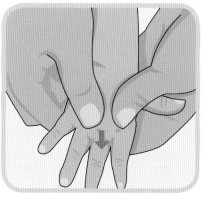

Apply gentle pressure.

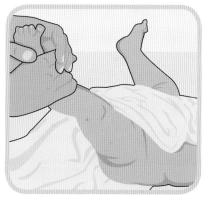

Work down thighs to calves.

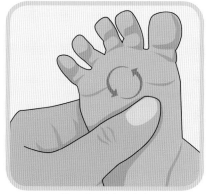

Move thumb in a circle.

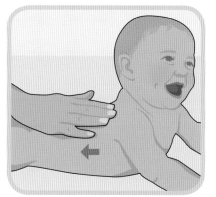

Stroke right side, then left.

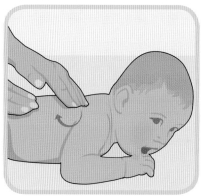

Make tiny fingertip circles.

91 care for the cord

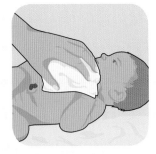

Keep it dry.

Stick to sponge baths.

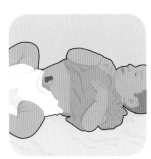

Keep it exposed to the air.

55 heal at home

Clean only if necessary.

Contact your pediatrician if there are signs of infection, such as redness, bleeding, or stinky discharge. If you do need to clean the stump, use only water, not alcohol.

92 sponge-bathe an infant

Wipe face from nose out.

Clean all skin folds.

Get between toes.

Shampoo with damp cloth.

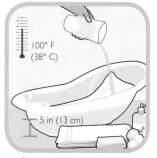
Prepare tub; gather supplies.

Support head and back.

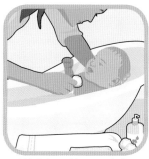
Wash face with cotton balls.

Wash body top to bottom.

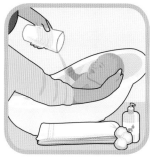
Add water to prevent chills.

Lean her over to wash back.

Wash her hair last.

sew a cute hooded towel 142

Dry and dress.

take baby's temperature 94

Lubricate the thermometer.

Lift legs. Talk or sing.

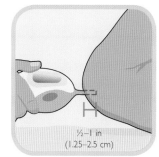
½–1 in
(1.25–2.5 cm)

Insert the thermometer.

Clean thermometer well.

95 trim baby's nails

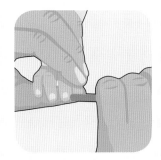

Wait for a calm moment.

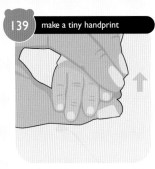

139 make a tiny handprint

Press pad away from nail.

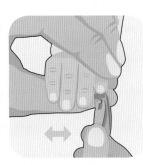

Cut a curved shape.

File any ragged edges.

96 clean baby's gums

Wrap a clean, damp cloth.

Hold baby close; tickle lip.

Gently rub top gums.

Repeat on the bottom.

Oral hygiene—it's not just for people with teeth! Make a habit of cleaning baby's gums after every feeding.

Massage olive oil into scalp.

Allow skin to absorb.

Gently remove scales.

Wipe with cloth; rinse well.

To remove scales, use only soft-bristled brushes.
Your fingers will also work just fine!

tackle tummy time **115**

  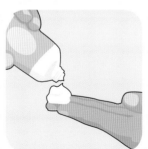  

Change diaper frequently.

Clean well and pat dry.

Use cream at every change.

Air out any flare-ups.

To clean, use unscented wipes or plain
water. See your doctor for severe rashes.

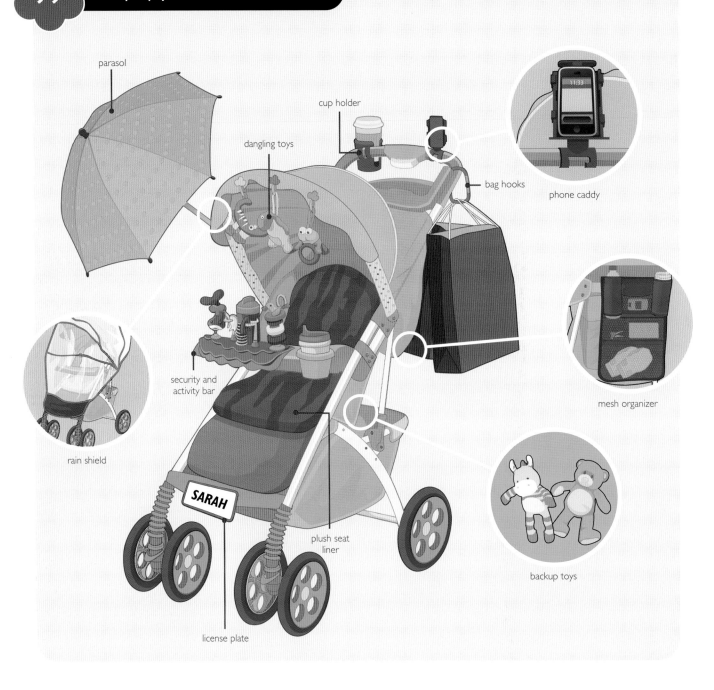

parasol

cup holder

dangling toys

phone caddy

bag hooks

security and
activity bar

rain shield

mesh organizer

SARAH

plush seat
liner

backup toys

license plate

Though it may be difficult to get to the gym with a young baby, you can fit a surprising amount of exercise into a park outing. Here are a few ideas to get you started.

Stretch out with a downward dog yoga pose.

Use baby's weight to work out your arms.

Gaze at baby and strengthen your core with mat exercises.

Get your pediatrician's permission to use a jogging stroller.

Help baby sit up while you tone your abdominals.

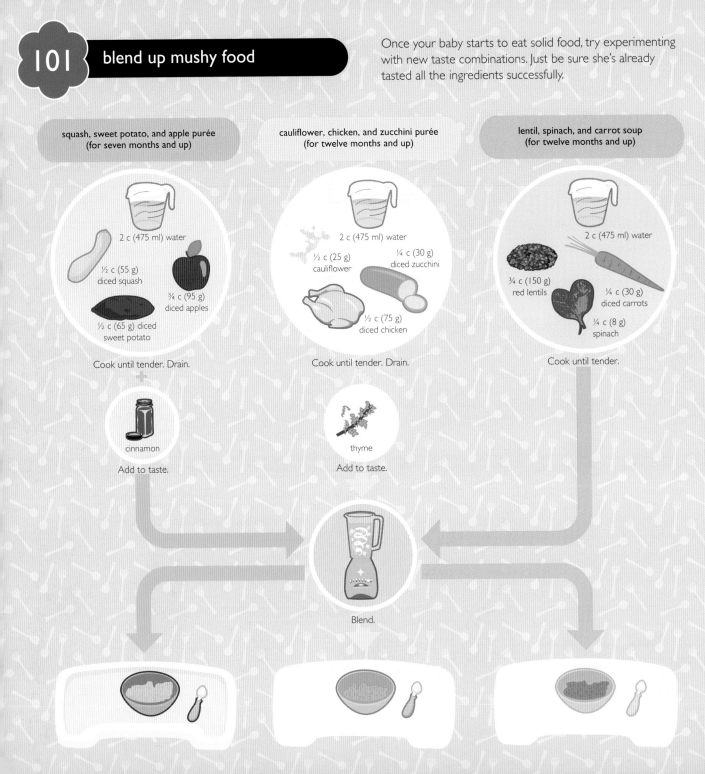

blend up mushy food

Once your baby starts to eat solid food, try experimenting with new taste combinations. Just be sure she's already tasted all the ingredients successfully.

squash, sweet potato, and apple purée
(for seven months and up)

2 c (475 ml) water

½ c (55 g) diced squash

¾ c (95 g) diced apples

½ c (65 g) diced sweet potato

Cook until tender. Drain.

cinnamon

Add to taste.

cauliflower, chicken, and zucchini purée
(for twelve months and up)

2 c (475 ml) water

½ c (25 g) cauliflower

¼ c (30 g) diced zucchini

½ c (75 g) diced chicken

Cook until tender. Drain.

thyme

Add to taste.

lentil, spinach, and carrot soup
(for twelve months and up)

2 c (475 ml) water

¾ c (150 g) red lentils

¼ c (30 g) diced carrots

¼ c (8 g) spinach

Cook until tender.

Blend.

Throw down a drop cloth.

Strap baby in his seat.

Cover up clothes.

Use two spoons.

Offer a sippy cup . . .

. . . and small bites.

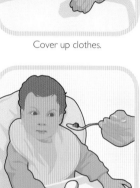

Let him be picky.

No luck? Try again later.

Cool cooked food.

Pour into ice-cube trays.

Freeze.

Double-bag; label and date.

At around nine months old, your baby can begin eating finger foods. Picking up bite-size bits of soft food (about the size of your pinkie nail) and getting them into her mouth is a fun challenge and helps develop fine motor skills and coordination.

Stock up on small containers and keep them filled with fresh snacks to grab on the go.

135 cut a puzzle sandwich

Healthy dips like applesauce, guacamole, hummus, and yogurt make mealtime fun.

*Cut everything into bite-size pieces.

Steam carrots and hard vegetables to soften them.

Dust slippery snacks (like fruit pieces) with whole-grain crumbs to help baby get a grip.

Keep servings small. Encourage grazing and offer choices.

*Though she may be feeding herself, it's still important to keep a close eye on your budding gourmand during meals.

Tip well!

Choose family-friendly spots.

Avoid peak mealtimes.

Use a place mat for finger foods.

Grab a booth or corner table.

Keep a favorite toy stashed for meltdown emergencies.

Buckle up for safety.

Pack quiet distractions like crayons and books.

Bring your own food, drink, and utensils.

Move objects out of reach.

take a car trip

Pack essential snacks, diapers, and toys.

Install a baby-view mirror.

Stick up a sunshade.

Provide some visual entertainment.

Talk, sing, or play music.

Take time out along the way.

*Car seats should be rear-facing until your baby is at least 1 year old and at least 20 lbs (9 kg). Keep it rear-facing up to the highest weight and height allowed by the seat's manufacturer.

trash bags

umbrella

hand sanitizer

diaper cream

wet wipes

extra clothes

diapers

adult shirts

sunblock

blankets

market bags

snacks

outdoor toys

indoor toys

baby wipes

bottled water

first-aid kit

adult pants

Use an approved car seat.

Check stroller at the gate.

Pack extra supplies.

Feed at takeoff.

Change in the bathroom.

Distract with new toys.

Take a walk if she's upset.

Feed during descent.

Combat new-mom exhaustion by taking time for yourself wherever you can grab it. Here are a few simple ways to slow down, feel better, and savor special moments.

Take time to fix your hair.

Find a minute for makeup.

Rest with your baby.

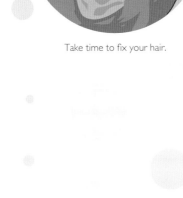

Soak in a relaxing bath.

Reach out; talk to friends and family.

Sit down to eat.

Go easy on yourself;
nobody can do it all.

Spend a moment alone to
walk, read, or meditate.

Live in the moment.
Laundry can wait.

Aromatherapy is a quick, effective, and pleasant stress-buster. Add a few drops of any of these oils to a diffuser or your bath water and take a deep breath.

ylang-ylang
soothes stress and anxiety

sandalwood
lifts mood and calms nerves

lavender
relieves pain and tension

Your baby, that sweet, drooling, captive audience, is going to find you the best show in town—just looking at you is endless amusement. Your facial expressions are a wonder! Your voice is thrilling! And the way you blow raspberries into his belly? A giggle fest. And the best part? Playing is learning. Every time you make a face, he's gaining understanding about his world. As he gets older, wiser, and more mobile you can expand your repertoire. Skip the expensive-toy aisle (that's for grandparents) and set about turning everyday objects into toys and everyday actions into opportunities for exploration. Yes, this means you're going to play approximately four million games of peekaboo and patty-cake, and push the park swing a few billion times, but remember, you get to play, too. Plus, on this go-around, you can reach the monkey bars. It's great to be a grown-up.

play

make baby laugh

Make faces. Shake your head. Add goofy noises.

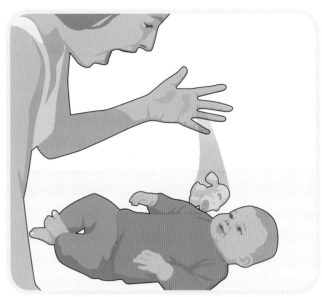

Drop soft toys with a "plop" or an "uh-oh!"

Taste his toes and talk in silly voices.

Blow raspberries and tickle his tummy with your nose.

Although babies start distinguishing colors at one week old,
high-contrast images like these are most visually stimulating.
Hang simple black-and-white pictures where baby can get a look.

Slowly wave bright toys.

prep the nursery   41

Hang high-contrast art.

Wear stripes!

Pull a toy past; let him track.

play with your baby

| 0–3 months | 3+ months | 6+ months | 9+ months |

airplane ride
eases colic; develops neck and shoulder strength

hammock time
promotes balance; builds back and neck strength

rolling a ball
helps balance; encourages movement and coordination

knocking blocks
refines motor skills; promotes shape recognition

rippling ribbons
boosts visual tracking and eye-hand coordination

noisemakers
fosters sound location; teaches cause and effect

nature walk
provides sensory experience

pillow obstacle course
nurtures body awareness; strengthens eye-foot coordination

---

114 roll up a boo-boo bunny

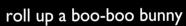

1 Lay a washcloth flat.

2 Roll it diagonally.

3 Bend the roll in half.

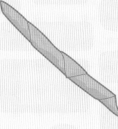

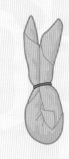

4 Secure with a rubber band.

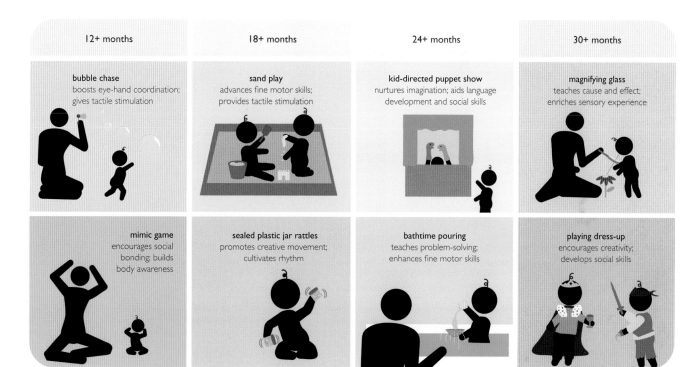

12+ months	18+ months	24+ months	30+ months
bubble chase boosts eye-hand coordination; gives tactile stimulation	**sand play** advances fine motor skills; provides tactile stimulation	**kid-directed puppet show** nurtures imagination; aids language development and social skills	**magnifying glass** teaches cause and effect; enriches sensory experience
mimic game encourages social bonding; builds body awareness	**sealed plastic jar rattles** promotes creative movement; cultivates rhythm	**bathtime pouring** teaches problem-solving; enhances fine motor skills	**playing dress-up** encourages creativity; develops social skills

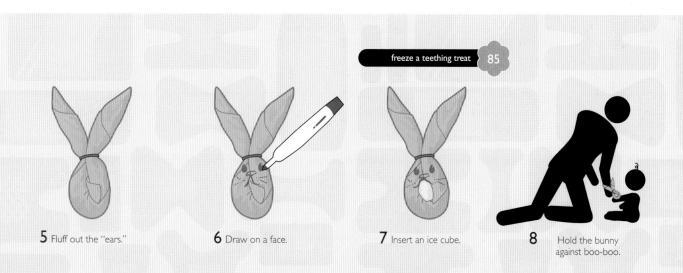

freeze a teething treat **85**

5 Fluff out the "ears."

6 Draw on a face.

7 Insert an ice cube.

8 Hold the bunny against boo-boo.

Prop baby up for a better view.

Make sure she has something to look at.

Get belly to belly (and nose to nose).

Give her a leg up.

Lie down for some face time.

53 hold a new baby

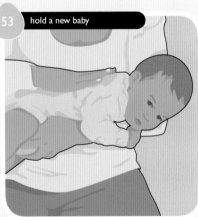

Drape baby over your arm.

Tummy time builds neck and torso strength. Your baby may find tummy time more enjoyable if she can look around, so try propping her up. If she's still cranky, don't keep her on her stomach for more than a few minutes each time.

promote sitting up | 116

1 Lay baby on your legs, holding his hands.

2 Let him pull up (with your help) to build sitting muscles.

encourage rolling over | 117

1 Place baby on a blanket or towel.

2 Lift the edge under his shoulder slowly.

strengthen with elbow stands | 118

1 Lay baby on a soft surface with her elbows under her shoulders.

2 To build crawling strength, slowly lift her hips and trunk, then lower.

support a wheelbarrow | 119

1 Wait until baby can lift her head and prop herself up on her arms.

2 Support her trunk and legs; hold for a slow count of three.

make a texture tag blanket

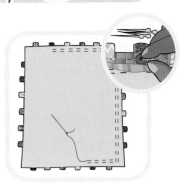

Gather fabric and ribbons.

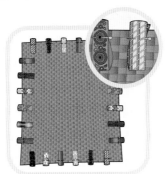

Pin ribbon loops to fabric.

Add second piece facedown.

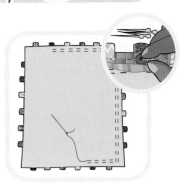

Stitch edges, removing pins.

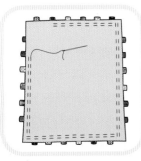

Leave one corner open.

Pull inside out.

Lay flat.

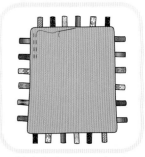

Stitch the last corner closed.

use a texture tag blanket

Lay it out at tummy time.

Cover up the cart.

87 troubleshoot sleeping issues

Use it to wind down.

Tuck in a friend.

Hide most of your body.

Search for musical toys.

Guess which cup it's under.

Put a lid on a favorite toy.

play peekaboo 123

Peek through your fingers.

Pop out with a smile.

Cover up with a blanket.

Let baby pull it off.

Cover baby's eyes.

Peekaboo!

Hide a toy behind you.

Peekaboo!

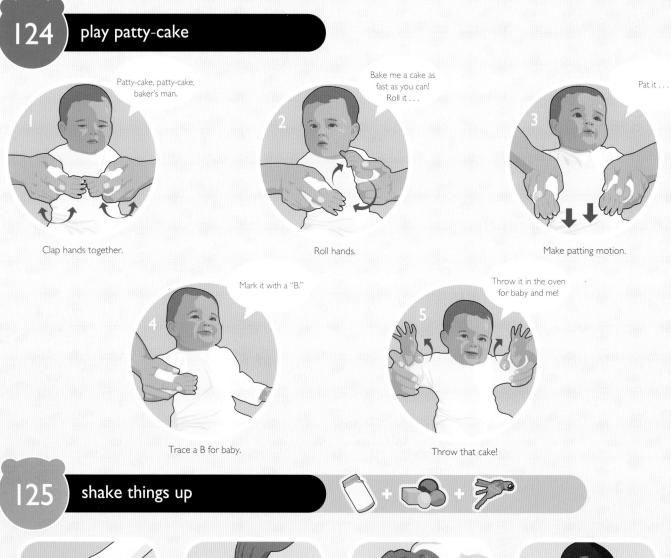

Patty-cake, patty-cake, baker's man.

1. Clap hands together.

Bake me a cake as fast as you can! Roll it . . .

2. Roll hands.

Pat it . . .

3. Make patting motion.

Mark it with a "B."

4. Trace a B for baby.

Throw it in the oven for baby and me!

5. Throw that cake!

125 shake things up

Clean a plastic container.

Partially fill with large objects.

Tightly close lid.

Shake it up, baby!

Make every day a dance party by adding music and movement to whatever you're doing. Tap out rhythms, sing, hum, dance, or play your favorite tunes.

fake a clean house 88

Swirl scarves for baby's entertainment.

Sway to classical music with your tiny dance partner.

Bounce to hip-hop.

Play some band tunes and march like a majorette.

Play a round of freeze dance.

Make up songs (and moves) for everyday chores.

Groove and get down.

Keep a beat with wooden spoons or other household objects.

Sing in silly voices—high, low, loud, and in a whisper.

127 help baby crawl

Lend a hand.

Put temptation out of reach.

Place toys at 10:00 and 2:00.

Make a tunnel.

 Setting toys just out of reach at these angles encourages a sitting baby to shift to one knee and reach forward—the same move that begins a crawl.

129 spot movement milestones

This is a general guide to movement milestones; keep in mind that your baby will learn to walk and crawl at her own pace.

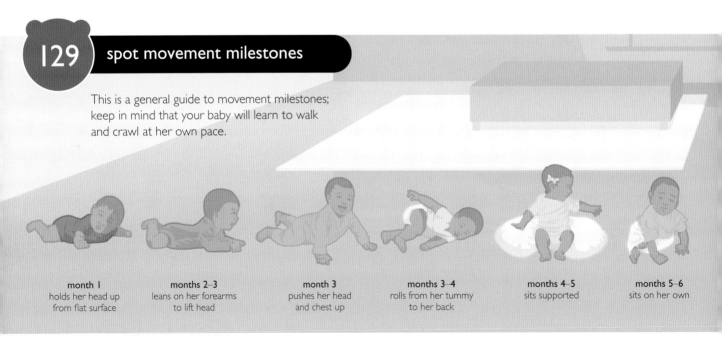

month 1
holds her head up
from flat surface

months 2–3
leans on her forearms
to lift head

month 3
pushes her head
and chest up

months 3–4
rolls from her tummy
to her back

months 4–5
sits supported

months 5–6
sits on her own

Give her something to push.

Support her torso. Cheer!

Take off her shoes.

Shine light for her to chase.

months 6–11
moves forward by scooting, creeping, or crawling

months 7–10
pulls up; walks holding on to furniture or push toys

months 10–14
stands alone

months 12–14
walks on her own

months 14+
walks well; can pull toys

130 distract baby at the store

Name the items you are buying. Talk about what you are doing.

Stimulate her senses by letting her smell and touch safe items.

1

Reward her patience with a fresh fruit treat.

Let baby drop unbreakables into the basket.

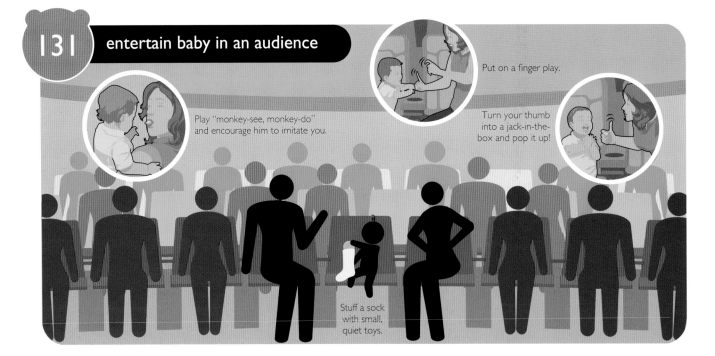

131 entertain baby in an audience

Put on a finger play.

Play "monkey-see, monkey-do" and encourage him to imitate you.

Turn your thumb into a jack-in-the-box and pop it up!

Stuff a sock with small, quiet toys.

Play a naming game. Ask her to point to parts of her face or body.

Hide a small toy in your pocket or sleeve and play hide-and-seek.

Entertain baby with a clapping game.

Hold her close and hum a tune.

Bring a toy phone so he can make important calls.

Unplug the keyboard and let him push buttons.

Hand over your keys.

Help him crinkle waste paper and put it into the recycling bin.

Peel a banana halfway.

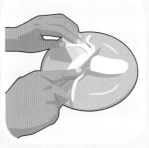

Cut off exposed fruit.

Snip the peel to make legs.

Position the banana upright.

Poke holes for the eyes.

Slice the banana.

nontoxic marker

Draw on a mouth.

feed finger foods 104

Serve!

Use soft fillings.

Press out shapes.

Arrange and serve.

Let him solve and eat!

Here's a sampling of items that can stimulate baby's sensory awareness. Hand them to her one at a time and supervise her closely.

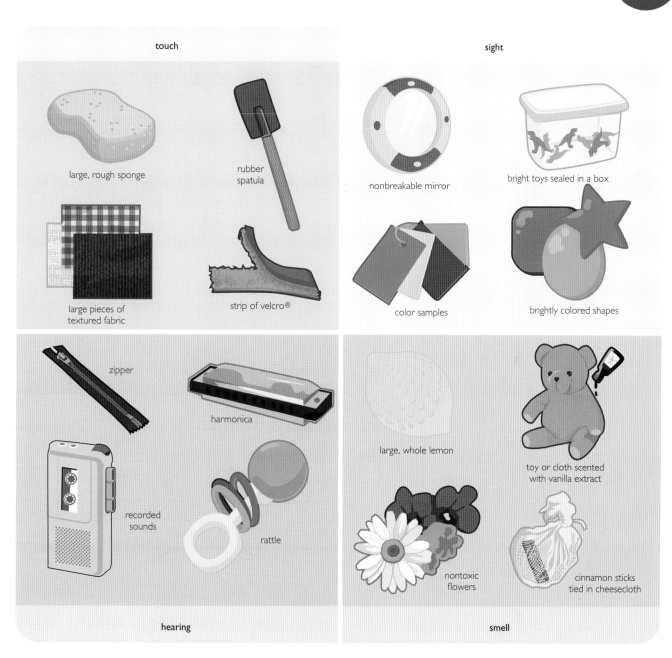

touch

large, rough sponge

rubber spatula

large pieces of textured fabric

strip of velcro®

sight

nonbreakable mirror

bright toys sealed in a box

color samples

brightly colored shapes

zipper

harmonica

recorded sounds

rattle

large, whole lemon

toy or cloth scented with vanilla extract

nontoxic flowers

cinnamon sticks tied in cheesecloth

hearing

smell

Slather on the sunscreen and meet some other parents and kids at the park. Very young children like to watch and play near but not with one another. Parents, however, definitely benefit from the companionship.

Support baby on the slide until he can sit up and feel confident.

Help your baby take turns.

Fill and spill buckets or bury toys in the sand for baby to find.

Bring extra toys to ease sharing issues.

To avoid meltdowns, give a warning before you have to leave.

Put your baby in a front pack and take him for a slow swing.

Keep a watchful eye on the children while you socialize.

Pack finger foods to share.

Play bubble chase on the grass with beginning walkers.

Throw down a drop cloth.

Tape a canvas to the table.

Clip on a dish towel.

Squeeze out some paint.

Show her how.

Watch her get creative.

Hang to dry.

Frame.

Paint with nontoxic paint.

Have paper ready.

Press down firmly.

44 decorate a nursery with stencils

Display proudly.

Tape plastic wrap to table.

Add color and shaving foam.

Tape plastic wrap on top.

Enjoy a no-mess squish.

Fill a dish with water.

Add brushes and sponges.

Paint paper, rocks, cement.

Let dry and try again!

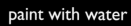

sew a cute hooded towel

Cut half circles from a towel.

Cut out four ear shapes.

Pair the ears; stitch together.

Pin ears between half circles.

Stitch edge, securing ears.

Turn inside out; pin in place.

Sew hood to towel.

93 bathe a baby

Insert baby.

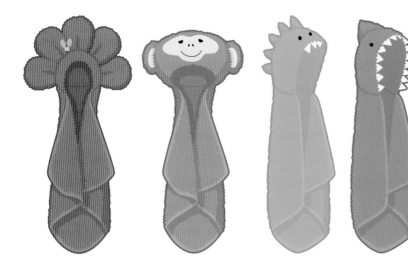

Blow bubbles.

Scoop, stir, and pour.

Go fishing for toys.

Pop up a duck.

Shower with a squirt bottle.

Try baby goggles for bathophobia.

Stick foam shapes to the tub sides.

Keep toys and supplies within arm's reach, and never leave baby unattended in the tub.

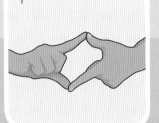

1

The itsy-bitsy spider . . .

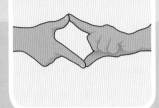

2

. . . climbed up the water spout.

3

Down came the rain . . .

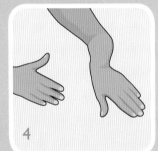

4

. . . and washed the spider out.

5

Out came the sun and
dried up all the rain.

6

And the itsy-bitsy spider
climbed up the spout again!

Use dark yarn for eyes.

Finish with a knot inside.

Stitch on an expression.

Attach a felt hair piece.

put on a puppet show 146

Tickle!

Name body parts.

Hang a blanket curtain and have a crib show.

102 manage mealtime

Act out moments of his day.

Make a stage and act out a familiar story complete with songs and silly voices.

Play hide-and-seek.

read with your baby

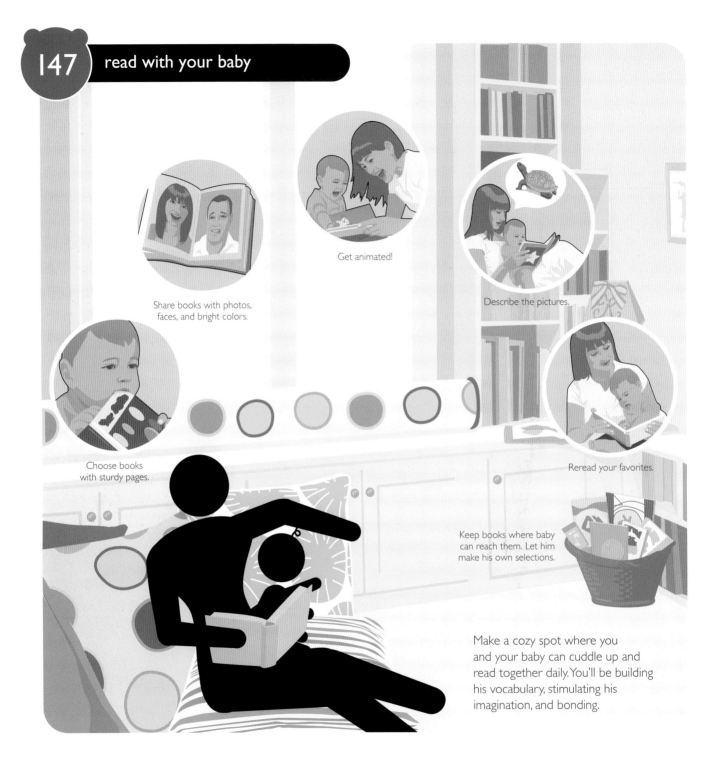

Share books with photos, faces, and bright colors.

Get animated!

Describe the pictures.

Choose books with sturdy pages.

Reread your favorites.

Keep books where baby can reach them. Let him make his own selections.

Make a cozy spot where you and your baby can cuddle up and read together daily. You'll be building his vocabulary, stimulating his imagination, and bonding.

Repeat consonant sounds.

Make eye contact; mimic.

Use gestures.

Narrate your actions.

Name the things you see.

Count.

Ask questions.

Play phone. Repeat words.

Scratch armpits.

Draw whiskers.

Open fingers like a beak.

Claw chest.

Listen to the rain making music on an umbrella.

Stop to look at the wet world up close.

Go ahead and get wet! You can dry off later.

Fix some warm treats when you get home.

Invite your shadow to the beach party!

Enjoy wading with your baby. Never leave baby unattended near any water.

Stay cool in the shade, and wear plenty of sunblock.

Pack a picnic lunch and remember to stay hydrated.

Catch falling leaves together.

Find a crunchy leaf bed and watch the autumn sky.

Collect treasures as you explore.

Kick up a leaf shower.

Catch snowflakes.

Make tracks and snow angels.

Take baby on a sled hike through the snow.

Build snow bricks in plastic kitchen containers.

Play parachute, build a fort, or put baby to work fluffing pillows.

Make sock puppets or play peekaboo with warm towels.

Have kids unload plastic dishes or match up pots and lids.

Little helpers can scrub, empty dustpans, or open junk mail.

Sit facing your baby.

Hold under her arms.

Ask if the flight crew is ready.

Three, two, one . . .

Count down for takeoff.

Roll back to blast off.

Keep eye contact.

Bring her in for a landing.

travel by air 108

Repeat. Stop if she is scared.

Hold baby facing you.

Grasp him under the arms.

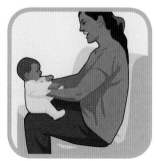

Sing; bounce to the rhythm.

Bounce lying down.

1 Seal box.

2 Cut seat and doors.

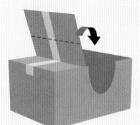

3 Score and fold windshield.

4 Cut out windsheld; tape.

5 Glue on plate wheels.

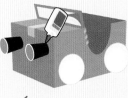

6 Attach cup lights.

7 Get a custom paint job.

8 Add upholstery.

106 take a car trip

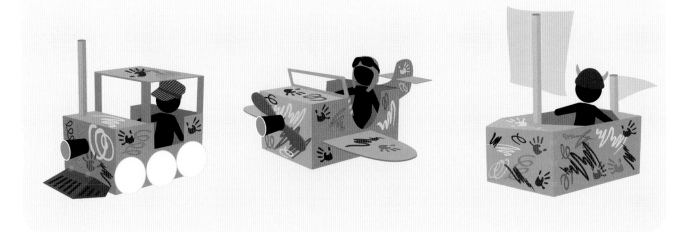

Make big, lightweight blocks from wrapped shoe boxes.

Stack up some blocks and let baby knock them down.

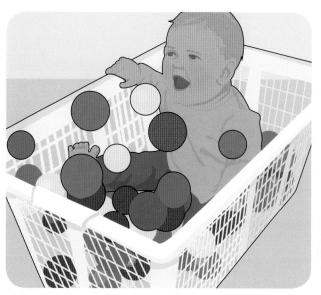

Put baby in a laundry basket with foam or plastic balls.

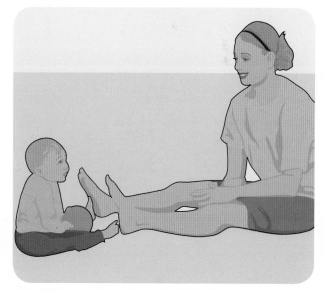

Make a corral by touching feet, then roll a ball back and forth.

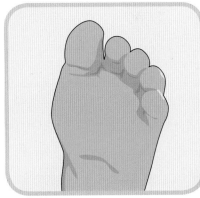

Capture details.

Use natural light.

Come down to his level.

Try black and white.

Go in for the close-up.

Get in the shot.

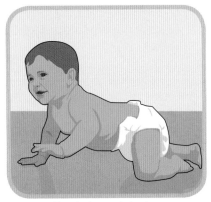

Keep backgrounds simple.

Take a few tasteful nudes.

Have your camera handy!

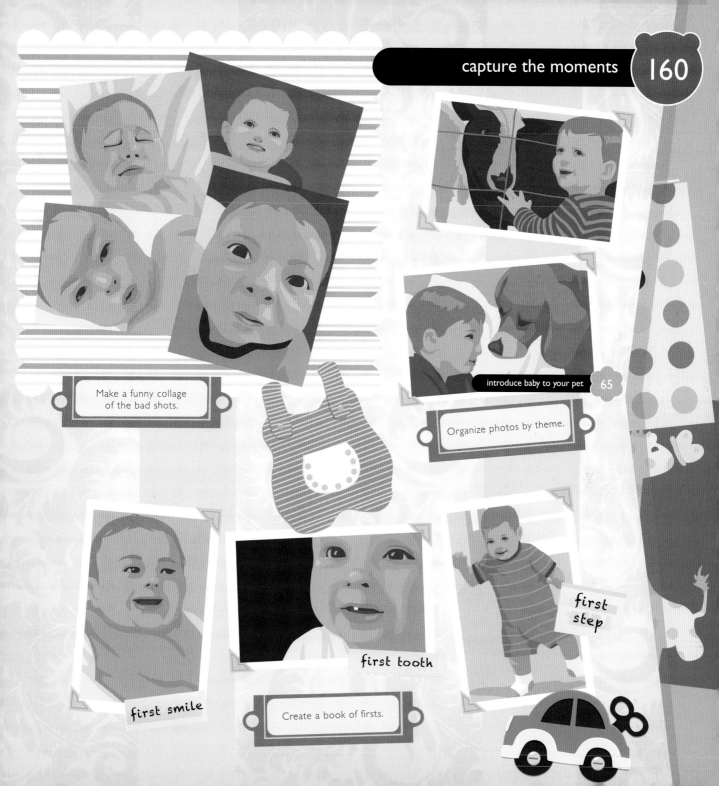

Make a funny collage of the bad shots.

introduce baby to your pet 65

Organize photos by theme.

first smile

first tooth

Create a book of firsts.

first step

161 swing with a retro baby

- traditional topper
- spiffy shades
- retro romper
- classic kicks

162 mosh with a punk baby

- faux hawk
- gothic one-piece
- black tutu
- skull-and-crossbones accessories

163 go green with an eco baby

- organic cotton lid
- soy-ink–printed shirt
- bamboo yoga pants
- sustainable shoes

164 chill out with a hippie baby

- tie-dyed hat
- mini dashiki
- crocheted pants
- hemp shoes

Cut the arms off
an adult-size shirt.

Fold baby pants in half.

Trace folded baby
pants onto sleeves.

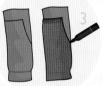

Cut along traced lines.

Fold fabric over elastic;
sew in place.

Separate legs; pin
elastic into waist.

Flip over; sew remaining
two layers together
to form crotch.

Pin and sew the top
two layers together.

Insert inside-out sleeve
into other sleeve.

Turn one sleeve inside-out.

Invite the people who have helped you all year.

Schedule the party to avoid nap time.

Feed the guest of honor ahead of time.

Designate a guest to capture the moment.

Serve kid-friendly snacks.

134 make a banana octopus

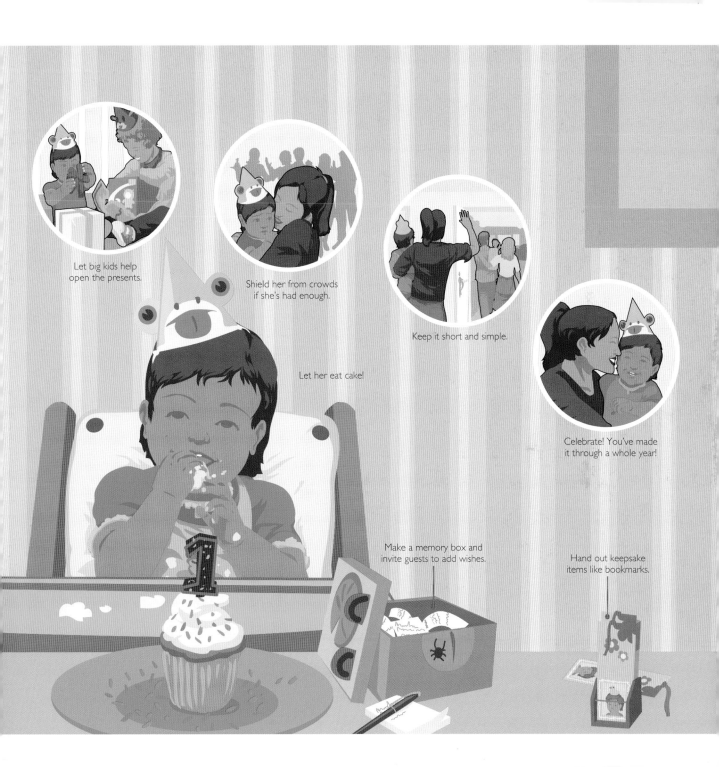

Let big kids help open the presents.

Shield her from crowds if she's had enough.

Keep it short and simple.

Let her eat cake!

Celebrate! You've made it through a whole year!

Make a memory box and invite guests to add wishes.

Hand out keepsake items like bookmarks.

tools

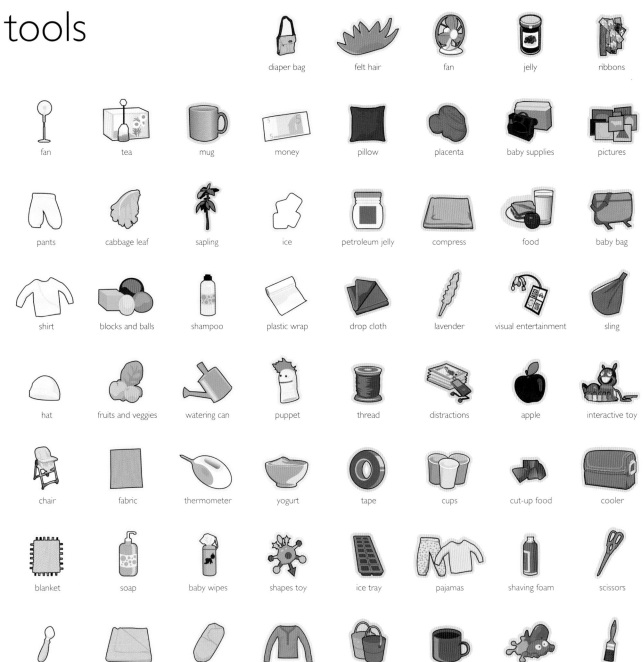

diaper bag · felt hair · fan · jelly · ribbons

fan · tea · mug · money · pillow · placenta · baby supplies · pictures

pants · cabbage leaf · sapling · ice · petroleum jelly · compress · food · baby bag

shirt · blocks and balls · shampoo · plastic wrap · drop cloth · lavender · visual entertainment · sling

hat · fruits and veggies · watering can · puppet · thread · distractions · apple · interactive toy

chair · fabric · thermometer · yogurt · tape · cups · cut-up food · cooler

blanket · soap · baby wipes · shapes toy · ice tray · pajamas · shaving foam · scissors

spoon · towel · swaddling blanket · sweater · buckets · beverage · creature toys · paint brush

sippy cup	car seat	pillow	goggles	yarn	bread	paint	pins
plaster of paris	antacid	diaper cream	jar	bear	pictures	sandwich	crayons
nail file	fleece	car toy	match	clove oil	basket	candles	duck
pig toy	skin cream	airplane toy	honey	cookies	plywood	clothespins	plush toy
bib	toothbrush	fish toy	brush	stencil brush	keys	sitz bath	string
cucumber and watermelon	monkey toy	ball toy	journal	towels	sponges	cracker	small meal
puppet	bear	ball	bear	picture frame	tape	banana	breast pump
diapers	baby oil	net	brush	box	wedge pillow	taxi	lanolin

plush toy	bandages	baby names	snack
pie tin	baby food	camera	flashlight
sock	baby soap	paper plates	olive oil
marker	nontoxic paints	food dye	pen
changing pad	drop cloth	paper	stencil
needle	stereo	dumbbells	scissors
window shade	frame	pen	baby tub
knife	paint tray	picture	low, wide heels
prenatal vitamin	finger food	cotton swab	cotton balls
cookie cutter	nail clippers	mirror	clock
ruler	bottle	blanket	pillows
shovel	vacuum cleaner	vermilion	fabric pen
elastic	white glue	baggies	nursing pads
portable stereo	pot	key	stroller bag
rubber band	paper towels	cup of water	belly support
spoon	trash can	table	box cutter

index

a-b-c

acupressure, inducing labor with 47
air travel with baby 108
airplane game 113, 155
animal signs game 149
aromatherapy 110
autumn outdoor activities with baby 152
baby development during pregnancy 13
baby food
  freezing 103
  recipe 101
baby handprint art 139
baby management
  in an audience 131
  in long lines 132
  at the office 133
  at the store 130
baby pictures
  scrapbook ideas 160
  tips 159
baby, preparation for 25, 41–45
ball games 158
banana octopus 134
baptism, orthodox 58
bathing a newborn 92–93
bathtub play 143
bedtime routine for baby 86
belly (see also bump)
  celebration of 39
  making a cast of 40
birth
  using self-hypnosis 29
  in water 27
birth announcement 66
birthday party for baby 166

blankets
  no-sew 43
  texture tag 120–121
blessing rituals for baby 57, 58, 60
block games 158
blocked duct, treatment for 74
bonding with newborn 50
bottle-feeding 76–77
bouncing-baby game 156
boxcar, how to build 157
boy baby, sexual positions to conceive 6
breast
  treatment for blocked duct 74
  treatment for engorgement of 73
breast engorgement, easing of 73
breast-feeding
  baby positions for 70
  description of 69
  on the go 71
breast-pump instructions 72
bubble play 113, 137, 143
bump (see also belly)
  concealing fashions for 24
  revealing fashions for 23
burping technique 78
car trip with baby 106–107
cat-cow pose for pregnancy 20
celebrations for baby
  blessing rituals 57, 58, 60
  chinese first-month 59
  first year 166
  naming rituals 61–62
cesarean section, description of 28
chamomile tea, for teething 85
chinese first-month celebration 59
cleaning house, quick method 88

clothes
  for baby 161–165
  for newborn 42
  for pregnancy 23–24
cobbler pose for pregnancy 21
colic, massage for 83
conception
  biological chart of 8
  planning for 4
  sexual positions for 5–7
cord (see umbilical cord)
cradle-cap treatment 97
crawling 127, 129
crying remedies 82–83

d-e-f

delivery (see also labor)
  epidural before 26
  preparation for 48
  in taxi 49
  using self-hypnosis 29
  in water 27
developmental chart
  for fetus 13
  for movement milestones 129
  for play skills 113
diaper bag 80
diaper-rash treatment 98
diapers
  changing technique 79
  solutions for disasters 81
discoloration on newborn 51
eating out with baby 105
egyptian naming ritual 62
elbow-stand exercise for baby 118
engorgement of breast, treatment for 73

7

3

27

41

48

epidural, description of 26
exercises for baby 115–119
fall outdoor activities with baby 152
fashions for baby
  eco 163
  hippie 164
  punk 162
  retro 161
feeding techniques for baby 102, 104–105
fertility cycle 4
fetal development
  chart of 13
  sonogram showing 14
finger foods for baby 104
finger painting 138
first birthday party 166
foods for baby 101, 103–104, 134–135

g-h-i

games for baby
  airplane 113, 155
  balls 158
  bouncing 156
  developmental chart for 113
  hide-and-seek 122
  housework 154
  itsy-bitsy spider 144
  knocking blocks 113, 158
  language-building 148
  laughter 111
  patty-cake 124
  peekaboo 123
gender of baby
  conception positions to influence 6–7
  divining technique for 38
  old wives' tales about 37

girl baby, sexual positions to conceive 7
gums
  care of 96
  and teething remedies 84–85
hammock game for baby 113
handmade blankets
  no-sew 43
  texture tag 120–121
handprint, baby 139
healing, post-partum 55
hindu naming ritual 61
holding techniques for newborn 53
home, baby-proofing of 45
homecoming, dressing baby for 52
hooded towel 142
hopi sunrise blessing 57
housecleaning, quick method 88
housework game 154
itsy-bitsy spider game 144

j-k-l

labor (see also delivery)
  inducing 46–47
  preparation for 48
language-building for baby 148
lanugo 51
laughter games for baby 111

m-n-o

make your baby laugh 111
massage
  for baby 90
  for colic 83
mealtime with baby 102, 105
meditation during pregnancy 34
milia 51

mimic game for baby 113
mongolian spots on baby 51
morning-sickness management 15
movement
  encouragement of 127–128
  milestones 129
  to music 126
  of unborn baby 36
nail trimming for baby 95
naming rituals for baby 57, 61–62
natural labor 27, 29, 46
nature walks with baby 113, 150–153
new mom
  healing tips for 55
  self-care for 109
  support network for 63
newborn
  bathing techniques for 92–93
  benign markings on 51
  bonding with 50
  homecoming clothing for 52
  how to burp 78
  how to hold 53
  stimulation for 54
nipples, healing cracked 75
nursery preparation and decoration 41, 44
nursing station 68
nursing tips 69–71
orthodox baptism 58
outdoor adventures with baby 113, 137, 150–153

p-q-r

packed bag
  for diaper changing 80
  for labor and delivery 48

42

65

101

80

104

painting
  finger 138
  handprint 139
  plastic-wrap technique 140
  with water 141
pampering tips for pregnancy 33
park workout for mom and baby 100
patty-cake game 124
pet introduction to baby 65
physical development of baby 115–119, 127–129
pictures
  scrapbook ideas 160
  tips for baby 159
pigeon pose for pregnancy 22
placenta, planting of 56
plane travel with baby 108
plastic-wrap painting 140
play chart, developmental 113
play with food
  banana octopus 134
  puzzle sandwich 135
playground activities for baby 137
playing dress-up 113
post-partum healing 55
pregnancy
  40-week plan 25
  avoiding unwanted touching during 30
  clothes fashions for 23–24
  how to share the news of 10
  meditation during 34
  nutrition guidelines for 11, 16, 18
  pampering yourself during 33
  preparation for 1–3
  remedies for aches and pains during 17
  remedies for indigestion during 18
  remedies for morning sickness during 15
  remedies for swelling during 16
  sex during 31–32
  signs of 9
  sleep comfortably during 19
  yoga poses during 20–22
public places, baby management for 105, 130–133
puppet, baby-sock 145
puppet show 113, 146
puzzle sandwich 135
reading to baby 147
red egg and ginger party 59
rituals for baby
  blessing 57, 60
  naming 57, 61–62
  orthodox baptism 58
roll-over exercise for baby 117

s-t-u

sandbox play 137
self-hypnosis birthing technique 29
sensory awareness 136
shoe boxes as blocks 158
sitting-up exercise for baby 116
sleeping recommendations
  for baby 87
  for pregnancy 19
sonogram, how to read 14
sponge bath for newborn 92
spring outdoor activities with baby 150
stencil decoration of nursery 44
stork bites, marking on newborn 51
stroller accessories 99
summer outdoor activities with baby 151
supermom-to-be, description of 12
support network for new mom 63
swaddling instructions 67

taxi, delivering a baby in 49
teething remedies 84–85
temperature, how to take baby's 94
texture tag blanket 120–121
towel, hooded 142
toys, handmade
  baby-sock puppet 145
  boo-boo bunny 114
  boxcar 157
  sensory box 136
  shaker 125
  shoe-box blocks 158
tummy exercise for baby 115
umbilical cord, care of 91
unborn baby
  connecting with 35
  gender of 37–38
  movement of 36

v-w-y

vernix 51
vision, early stimulation of 112–113
visitors
  baby-safety tips for 64
  quick housecleaning tips before 88
walk, learning to 128–129
water birth, description of 27
water painting 141
water play at bathtime 143
wheelbarrow exercise for baby 119
winter outdoor activities with baby 153
workout for mom and baby 100
yoga poses
  with baby 89
  during pregnancy 20–22
yoruba baby blessing 60

163   105   147   137   88

show me who

weldon**owen**

415 Jackson Street
San Francisco CA 94111
www.wopublishing.com

CEO, President Terry Newell

VP, Sales and
New Business Development Amy Kaneko

VP, Publisher Roger Shaw

Creative Director Kelly Booth

Executive Editor Mariah Bear

Editor Lucie Parker

Project Editor Frances Reade

Editorial Assistants Emelie Griffin,
Katharine Moore

Senior Designer Stephanie Tang

Designers Meghan Hildebrand, Rachel Liang

Illustration Coordinator Conor Buckley

Production Director Chris Hemesath

Production Manager Michelle Duggan

Production Coordinator Charles Mathews

Color Manager Teri Bell

parenting magazine

2 Park Avenue
New York NY 10016
www.parenting.com/store

Editorial Director Ana Connery

Executive Editors Shawn Bean and
Elizabeth Anne Shaw

Copyright © 2011 by Weldon Owen Inc.
All rights reserved. Unauthorized reproduction, in
any manner, is prohibited.

Parenting and Weldon Owen are divisions of
BONNIER

Library of Congress Control Number: 2010941175

ISBN: 978-1-61628-112-0

10 9 8 7 6 5 4 3 2
2014 2013 2012 2011

Printed in China by 1010

Special thanks to:

Storyboarders
Sarah Duncan, Sheila Masson, Jamie Spinello,
Brandi Valenza, Astrea White, Kevin Yuen

Illustration specialists
Hayden Foell, Jamie Spinello, Ross Sublett

Editorial and research support team
Kendra DeMoura, Alex Eros, Jann Jones, Marianna
Monaco, Gail Nelson-Bonebrake, David Sackrider,
Denise Schipani, Marisa Solîs, Mary Zhang

Extra thanks to Elizabeth Dougherty for her expert
review of the content.

A **Show Me Now** Book.
Show Me Now is a trademark
of Weldon Owen Inc.
www.showmenow.com

ILLUSTRATION CREDITS The artwork in this book
was a true team effort. We are happy to thank and
acknowledge our illustrators.

Front Cover: **Britt Hanson:** info people **Tina Cash Walsh:**
massage baby, book

Back Cover: **Tina Cash Walsh:** induce labor, trim nails
Christine Meighan: paint under plastic

Key bg=background, fr=frames

Juan Calle (Liberum Donum): 1, 2, 5, 11, 12, 30, 31, 32,
40, 45, 57, 58, 59, 60, 61, 62, 109 fr, 130 fr, 131 fr, 132
fr, 133 fr, 137, 161, 162, 163, 164, 166 **Hayden Foell:**
15, 48, 103 **Britt Hanson:** 34, 42, 67, 81, 88, 100, 113,
143 bg, 150, 151, 152, 153 **Rachel Liang:** 4, 8 **Christine
Meighan:** 68, 104, 125, 135, 139, 140, 142, 145, 146
extra art **Paula Rogers:** 9, 16, 53, 54, 64, 65, 79, 84, 85,
90, 91, 92, 115, 158 **Jamie Spinello:** 23, 24, 37, 55, 56,
69 bg, 70, 109 bg, 126 **Ross Sublett:** 25 **Stephanie**

Tang: 36 **Bryon Thompson:** 13, 20, 21, 22, 89, 114, 116,
117, 118, 119, 130 bg, 131 bg, 132 bg, 133 bg, 157
Lauren Towner: 3, 10, 33, 86, 112, 127, 128, 129
Gabhor Utomo: 26, 27, 28, 29, 35, 38, 39, 41, 49, 50,
51, 52, 63, 66, 69, 82, 87, 102, 105, 108, 110, 111, 121,
122, 123, 124, 134, 138, 141, 143 fr, 146 fr, 147, 148,
149, 154, 155, 156, 159, 160 **Tina Cash Walsh:** 17, 18,
19, 46, 47, 71, 72, 73, 74, 75, 76, 77, 78, 80, 83, 93, 94,
95, 96, 97, 98, 106 **Mary Zins:** 43, 44, 99, 120, 144, 165